D0569591

The **Oldie**
BOOK OF CARTOONS

The best thing about living alone is you can watch the telly without switching it on

GED

The Oldie
BOOK OF CARTOONS

Chosen by
Alexander Chancellor

This edition published by Oldie Publications Ltd in 2015

First published in 2015
by Oldie Publications Ltd

65 Newman Street, London W1T 3EG
www.theoldie.co.uk

Copyright © 2016 Oldie Publications Ltd

ISBN-13: 978-1-901170-24-5

A catalogue record for this book
is available from the British Library

Printed in the UK by St. Ives Group

Introduction

THERE IS an astonishing number of cartoonists – or would-be cartoonists – in this country. Hundreds of unsolicited cartoons pour into *The Oldie*'s office every month, and of these we can publish only a few, even though we use more than most other magazines. I sometimes wonder why cartoonists don't lose heart when so much of their work is rejected, but there seems to be an urge to share a drawing and a joke with the rest of the world that no amount of disappointment can quench.

Thankfully, this means that there are an awful lot of cartoons for us to choose from, so there are always some that we like. The choice is, of course, a subjective one, and we wouldn't expect all readers to agree with our decisions. But we hope there are enough to amuse at least some of you some of the time.

The hardest thing is to find cartoons in which the drawing and the joke are of equal quality. This is not something that is often achieved. Even so, there are always enough cartoons to raise a smile, or a stab of recognition, in me at any rate. Strangely, I tend to find that the least successful cartoons are those that deal with contemporary problems or trends, and not just things like the migration crisis or the iniquities of Isis, which don't lend themselves easily to humour: most jokes about smartphones, tweeting, selfies and so on also have a tendency to fall flat.

Better are the classical cartoon backdrops that have proved themselves suitable for an almost limitless variety of jokes – the desert island, the grim reaper, the psychiatrist's couch, the job interview, the courtroom, the cocktail party, and so on. There are plenty of these in this collection, and they remain fine vehicles for observations on the absurdity of the human condition.

ALEXANDER CHANCELLOR

'Ignore him, he's after scraps'

'Another 500 quid ensures
that the pall-bearers look
suitably mournful'

'Ooh look – Timmy has sent his first letter
from boarding school'

'Would you like mummy to download a
bedtime story to your iPod?'

'You should have known I meant "left" when I said right'

'It's the car park on CCTV. I missed last night's episode'

'She wants to speak to the organ grinder'

'I preferred his earlier work'

'Don't call me, text me, email me, visit my blog,
join me on Facebook or follow me on Twitter'

'You'll get up first thing in the morning and clean it all off'

'So you're his fancy woman!'

'Your screams may be recorded for training purposes'

'I'm afraid Bob's not your Uncle any more'

'Frankie, you're not supposed to see me on our
wedding day!'

'Got anything in gangland?'

'It's nice to see a bit of honesty creeping back into banking at last'

PLEASE WAIT HERE TO COMPLAIN ABOUT HAVING TO WAIT HERE

'It's alright for you. You won't have to go through the grieving process'

'It's ten o'clock. Normally I'd be in a meeting with Bradley from Accounts,
followed by a session with Harrison from Forward Planning'

'Eye of newt, wing of bat . . .
oh sod it, let's open a tin'

'I further suggest that while at school you
soaked a conker in vinegar'

'We have CCTV footage of your entire life'

'You did? At your age?'

'I've wired the email to the toaster'

'You've mastered the "Stay Calm" part.
Could we see some "Carry On"?'

'Scissors – I win'

'These days I do most of
my shoplifting online . . .'

'I'll take it'

'I would now like to read out a few text messages . . .'

'Careful! You could put an eye out
with that thing'

'Let's face it, Gerald. A late flowering is the best
you can hope for'

'Right, Syd – programme the
satnav for Brighton'

'I've been shopping all day – my fingers are killing me'

'All right – tomorrow you park'

'They've developed a very sophisticated form of communication'

'He had a hop-on part in a David Attenborough Special'

'Can you sex it up a bit?'

'Next time remember to put the lid back on the superglue!'

'How do you plead . . .
framed or unframed?'

'Turner, don't use that expression
"Pie in the sky" – it sounds
ridiculous – and don't point!'

'I loved the book, but some changes are needed: a boob job – 40B would be
good – shorter skirt, high heels, more make-up and some dental work'

'Sorry I'm late. What with Thursday being the new Friday, I thought it was Saturday'

'I have this strange attraction to people who don't like me

'Oh look, a Crested Newt'

'Can I get you anything from the pharmacy, sir?'

'I'm afraid I can't discuss individual cases'

'I'm new in town – do you know where one registers as a sex offender?'

'Sorry we'd like to try that again'

'Do you ever wish you were a cuckoo?'

'Now my personal favourite: Market research shows a very positive response from the general public to this image'

'On a day like this, one hardly needs nipple clamps'

PARALYTIC GAMES

'Permission to write some poetry, Sir?'

'I thought we could freeze it . . .'

'You have the right to remain silent . . .'   'What goes with flaming argument?'

'Must do Munch'

'Not guilty, Fred'

'Caught anything?'

'You've caught us at a bad time. Can I call you back?'

BILL PROUD

'He's a tortured genius – I make sure of that'

YOU'RE SIXTY AND YOU'VE NEVER SOLD A PAINTING. SELF-MUTILATION IS YOUR ONLY HOPE

'I always knew you would grow old gracefully, Eric, but I was rather hoping there would be one or two disgraceful highlights . . .'

'Your mother's got to carry on working as long as I live'

'Would you like me to throw that in the river for you, sir?'

'We've been born into a surveillance society

33

'They leave a radish on your pillow'

'I'm sorry, Henderson – we're going to have to let you go'

'The invitation says CASUAL DRESS, what's that?'

'I'll have what he had'

'Now, now, Henderson – that will have to wait until "Any Other Business"'

'So she said, "Either that shed goes or I go"'

'I envy you your unshakeable belief in life after extinction!'

'I've got sand everywhere'

'It's simple: you bully me, I sue, and we split the damages'

'It was an assisted suicide'

'And how long have you felt
inferior, Mother Superior'

'How do you slip "What's your favourite hymn?" into the conversation?'

'You're on television? Would I have seen you in anything?'

'Today the bear is grizzly'

'And don't forget to act rich'

'There's no need to switch off your
mobile phones!'

'The double deluxe gets both of you upstairs before you can forget why you're going'

'We tend to favour traditional forms of anaesthetic here'

'OMG! They must be Boris dancers!'

'You think you've got problems'

'You're aloof, distant and condescending
– we're moving you into management'

'Is anything up with Gerald?
He seems a bit distant'

'Have you seen my invisible hearing aid?'

DIGNITAS

'Does it contain nuts?'

'See anything?'

ALL TRAINS CANCELLED

ADVERSE WEATHER CONDITIONS SHAKER

'Remember the good old days when we were the opium of the masses?'

43

44

'But **you** were supposed to catch **me**!'

'So when does the feeling kick in?'

'I'm going to lie on a towel, eat food and drink beer, of course I'm beach ready'

you've forgotten
you already came back
for what you forgot

45

'Wi-fi . . . wi-fi . . .'

'Leave it out, woman, you're doing my head in!'

'The new vicar's very much a traditionalist'

'"Long ago far away . . ." Libel laws probably prevent them from being more specific'

'Hurry up! It's that awful woman you can't stand'

'That's right, officer, my husband has just pre-deceased me . . .'

47

'Do you think they'll ever rise up and try to overthrow us?'

'Here comes the bill'

'I'm the bridesmaid'

'And it shall come to pass, Great Caeser, you shall have a salad named after you'

'Frankly, your bum looks big in anything'

'I just wish you would shut up sometimes and let someone else get a word in'

'No, the last one is the church's wifi password'

'Here's a March special – a five-day "Scatter his Ashes" cruise'

'You complete bastard!'

'Come on, Dad. you should make an effort to understand the new technology'

'Dad, what's an envelope?'

MEDICAL CENTRE

PLEASE PLAN
YOUR ILLNESS
TWO WEEKS
IN ADVANCE

'Have you any idea how many sea turtles have been trapped in shrimp nets while we've
been enjoying ourselves?'

'Hi, I'm in a two-minute silence . . .'

The first telephone cable

'The thin man inside you who has always been trying to get out is now also clinically obese'

'. . . and what did the barber say when you called him thick?'

'And how long have you had these feelings of being aboninable?'

'I think I'll check on how Bob's presentation went'

IT'S MORE HUMBLE

—SIT.

'Right, lads – into the woods and cut yourselves selfie sticks'

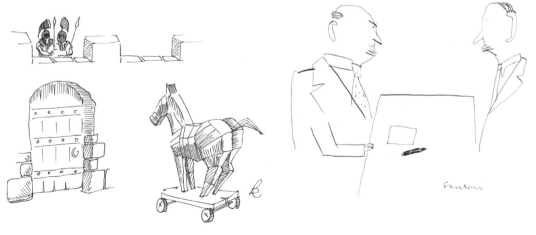

'Oh look, a horse. I love horses, let's bring it in'

'I liked it better, Henderson, when
you thought inside the box'

'Local character with a fund of interesting stories. Buy me a pint and I'll clear off'

'I'm the only deity this house requires'

'Your Mother's a keen supporter of assisted suicide'

'I knew this fracking would cause problems'

'Uh-oh, fly topping. You've given me
Spiderman's order again'

'Looks like we're eating in
again tonight'

'General. I come to ask you for your
son's hand in marriage'

'Decisions, decisions . . .'

'We feel the less said about this one the better'

'Did you lock the back door?'

Just what makes you tick?

my pacemaker

GED

YONDER HENCE

'The genetic tests show you're not a swan, kid. You're
just a really ugly duckling'

65

'It's just an ordinary 300 up, 300 down'

'Hang on while I tweet that I'm telling you
to hang on while I tweet'

67

Archbishop of Cadbury

'Oh, come on – you didn't expect "woof" to be still available as a password?'

'You've got to hand it to him, he does it twice a day, regular as clockwork . . . It's no wonder they made him king'

'Come on, Dr Watson, haven't you got Holmes to go to?'

'What's wrong, darling? You're taking a long time to make a fool of yourself'

'You spoil that giraffe'

when I get out
I'm gonna go straight, ma

'If you're happy and you know it clap your hands'

'I'm under stress, Miss Gibson. Come in and bite my nails'

'Maybe it's nature's way of telling you to slow down?'

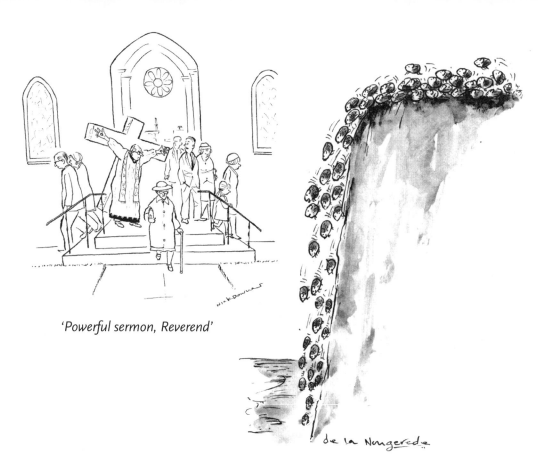

'Powerful sermon, Reverend'

'I hate the mad rush to the seaside'

'Do you have any pigs' hearts?'

'Alf, I don't know what this company would do
without you but we're going to give it a go!'

'We sat on that bench last year'

'Well, I suppose you could try Farrow and Ball. I believe they have a rather attractive
Autumn range out at the moment'

'That's typical of this airline – our luggage has been washed up on a different island'

'He's tunnelled out!'

'It's the big cheese. He's in a pickle'

'OMG. She's laying the fish knives out'

'Now, what did I come in here for?'

'WICKED!'

'He's the local no-frills undertaker'

'Are we nearly there yet, Dad?'

'I'm sorry I don't have any form of identification.
Isn't being your husband enough?'

'We don't know if it's a boy or girl yet.
It can make that decision for itself when
it's old enough'

'What time would you like the cockerel to wake
you in the morning?'

'Ah, Mozart's "Eine Kleine Liftmusic"'

He got up early to see the sunset.

'Now I'm not sure if it wasn't better how we had it in the first place'

'A packet of salt 'n' vinegar
crisps, barman, and have
one for yourself!'

'Arnold – it's the piano tuna'

'I heard you were available'

'Have you seen my toupee anywhere?'

'I heard that!'

'I'm not sure if I told you this, Oliver,
but warts and all will be extra'

'The Mitchells' costume party – I suppose
you'll be going as a pirate again?'

'Thank you for choosing this pavement. We
hope you have had a pleasant journey'

'There's no easy way to tell you this – you've got a nut allergy'

Bigissue! Bigissue! Blessyo Blessyou!

'If you want to smirk, Roger, go outside'

'Don't panic – he always feigns death when it's his round'

'Tyndale's not on till three – I'm just the warm-up act'

'. . . and you must be Sleazy!'

'What would I recommend?
Well, Vesuvio's over the road
is very good'

'. . . and when you wake up you'll believe
my fees to be extremely reasonable'

'It seems you're having trouble accepting the futility of existence'

'Goodnight, Nanook. Great housewarming party'

'The trouble with this country is that all the people who know how to run it are too busy driving taxis or cutting hair'

'You do realise that this religious symbol could cause offence?'

Mummy, why are your hands so soft?

I used to model for Salvador Dali, darling.

'It's nothing personal – I'm a psychopath'

'Well, Mr Jones, as you didn't die, we now have a small problem of bed shortage . . .'

'. . . and this is your blood-pressure warning light'

'Agnes is leaving me for someone with more air miles'

'When did you opt for a downshift in lifestyle?'

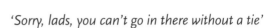

'Sorry, lads, you can't go in there without a tie'

'I've changed the way I shop'

'I vote we refuse to strike'

'I suggest my learned friend is neither
learned nor a friend'

'It's good to get away from the office . . .'

ANY CHANGE?

NO – I'M STILL THE SAME TIGHT-FISTED BASTARD

'Have you noticed how the security guards seem to follow you around the room?'

'You never plead with me to stay like you used to'

'As you can see, we have neighbours from Hell'

'More E, vicar?'

'Hold on, I need to check my p-mail'

'I thought we came here to relax?'

'I hear he's filthy rich'

'Now enter a six in that little box'

'It'll be a typical Japanese meal I expect – we'll be hungry an hour later'

'Mildred, could you not be the last thing I see before I die?'

'This episode calls for your resentful anger. Oh and I hear
they'll not be renewing your contract'

'Oh come on, Barney – everybody's online and tweeting these days!'

'How should I know if they hurt?! I ain't kicked anyone with them yet!'

'George, do you mind if we don't have the puppet show tonight? I'm so tired'

'Take no notice, Susan, he's at that inquisitive age'

'Everything's me-me-me with you people'

'I can't stand this foreign muck – gimme pizza or a curry any day!'

'Sky has given us a far greater choice of programmes to switch off'

'That's the financial district'

'Dad, I couldn't sleep, so I hacked into the US missile system . . .'

'I've got two tickets for the Rolling Stones
if you're interested!'

'I've forgotten what my famous last words were going to be'

LIFTS TO FLATS

'If only they had mobile phones . . .'

'Would you mind accompanying me to the police station, sir? Only this is a very rough area'

'Don't you think you're a bit overdressed for a first date?'

'The funeral business has been good to me'

'The last time I was here they taught me to
read and write – now I'm in for forgery'

'It works every time!'

'Haven't I seen you on television?'

'Dad, why are we called "Travellers"?'

'Who's a pretty boy, then?'

'Do you think we ought to tell them?'

'I like it'

'First let them try their hand at pronouncing it – THEN tell them it's off'

'One please'

'. . . I haven't seen you at church recently'

'No one leaves the class until I find out
who's responsible for this'

'Have you considered opera?'

'Hmm, impressive CV . . .'

'Do you **have** to hum?'

'I see the housing market is picking up'

'Don't worry. I've been married for 35 years so I'm used to turbulence'

'Right hand down a bit'

'OK! You can treat me privately . . .'

'Bloody dawn chorus'

'Mum, Dad – this is Kevin. Kevin works in advertising'

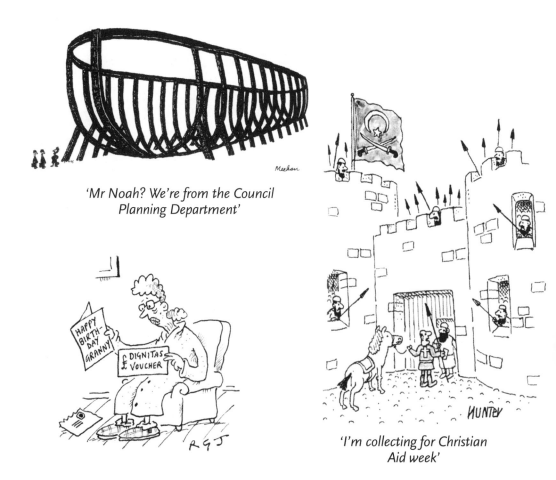

'Mr Noah? We're from the Council
Planning Department'

'I'm collecting for Christian
Aid week'

'Nigel persuaded his parents to move nearer so he could keep an eye on them'

'Are you sure there isn't, Edith?'

'I can't really talk now. I'm
being chased by a bull'

'Why don't you just get a
mobile phone then people
won't think you're weird?'

'Don't read too much into it, Mr Perkins, it's
just a hole in the roof'

'So you're a cartoonist too?'

'He's going clubbing'

'I wish to enrol for the chattering classes'

'It's lovely, darling, but you're not allowed to draw the prophet Mohammed'

'They've been roosting there for a couple of years now . . .'

'Before we start, why don't we go round and each say a little something about ourselves?'

'Congratulations! You've won the Oldie of the Year!'

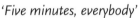

'Five minutes, everybody'

'I'll have the five loaves and two fishes'

'Did you pack your own luggage?'

'Could you spare a cup of Valium?'

'Trouble is, I don't know how much longer we can maintain this lifestyle'

'Thank you – that'll be all'

'You could at
least leer
occasionally'

'Hurry up – I've only got time for a soundbite'

'Alf, I don't know what this company would do without you but we're going to give it a go!'

'...apparently Norfolk's the new Suffolk'

'Can you hang on until I move my BMW, Wilsher?'

'All right, what's the first thing we check after the stereo being on full blast?'

'You're going on a long journey'

'Go on, you can do it!
Think misery'

'That's our winter fuel allowance well spent'

'Living gods don't wear zip-up cardis'

'Waiter, there's some soup in his hair'

'I can't see the point of all these
damn meetings'

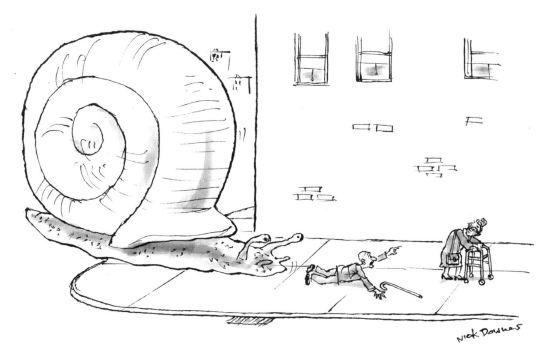

'Go on without me – save yourself!'

'I still say climate change is a hoax'

'We're looking for a person with "get up and go". Now we want you to get up and go'

'Excellent! Now try it again, but maybe a little earlier on the brake'

'Here come the suits'

'Whose turn is it to start tonight's argument?'

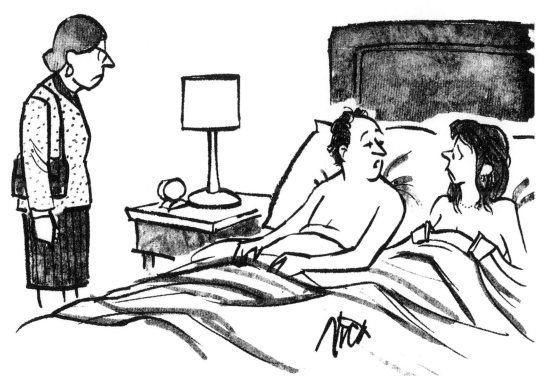

'You're in charge of scheduling, Jessica – how long has this been going on?'

'And here's one I made earlier . . .'

'. . . And you have two minutes on your chosen subject – the life and times of Christine Keeler'

'Lost cat . . .'

BANKING

'Hang on! Somebody's not cheating!'

'We call it placebo surgery. It doesn't work but it's a lot cheaper'

'One day Rover

'No, I'm afraid it's not not a D-Day
ceremonial fly-past, Your Majesty,
It's your air force'

'Have you got anything that smells of success?'

'Where do you see yourself in five minutes time?'

'When I grow up I hope to be an iconic
example of the misspent life'

'We're never going to lure them on to the rocks with you looking like that'

'It's good to get out of uniform'

'Before we go, could you cut the hedge?'

'It's from the police thanking me for helping them with their enquiries'

THE PERSON YOU
ARE CALLING KNOWS
YOU ARE WAITING

'. . . I know all about art but I don't know what I like'

'It's funny – everyone always remembers where they were when Humpty Dumpty had a great fall'

'Go to sleep, dear, or the childcare professionals will come and get you'

149

'As to the charge of illegal entry, the accused would like 58, 943, 762 similar offences to be taken into account'

'Did you say this was your first Christening?'

'You've developed what we call "Tweeter's Stoop"'

'When we went to bed last night she was a rather ugly princess'

'I'm sexing up my confessions'

'Who shall I say is ceawling?'

'I want to know everything about you, Michael. What facial hair cleanser you use, moisturiser, hairgel, exfoliator . . .'

'If I've told you once I've told you a thousand times – don't exaggerate'

'That's a pretty kettle of fish'

'Don't try anything or I'll sue you for resisting a burglary'

'If you begin to feel unwell, start or stop taking the aspirin'

'Please don't put your coffee on the coffee table'

'I've got a job for you, Penbury
– I want you to go out and look
for one!'

'I caught her running away to join the
media circus'

'I find you get much better coverage from the broadsheets'

'I didn't realise you had step-children, Henry'

Glossary of cartoonists

A J Singleton
Aaron
Addison
Alan Ralph
Alexei Talimonov
Bailey
BB
Barry Knowles
Beck
Bernie
Bill Proud
Bill Tidy
Birch
Blot
Bob
Bob Wilson
Boyce
Burton
Caz
Chris Madden
Christopher Mackenzie
Clive Collins
Cluff
Colin Wheeler
Colin Whittock
Cookson
Cooper
Cox
Cramer
Darling
de la Nougerede
Dish
Dredge
E Smith
Fantoni

Feggo
Freiesleben
Ged
Generer
Geoff Horton
Geoff Thompson
George Craig
Gf
Goddard
Gordon Gurvan
Grain
Grizelda Grizlingham
G T Riach
Ham Khan
Hawker
Holland
Honeysett
Hugh Burnett
Hunter
Ian Baker
Ines
Ivor
Jacob
Jag
Jan
Jelliffe
John Lightbourne
Jonesy
Jorodo
K J Lamb
Kelly
Ken Pyne
Kleh
KMS
Knife

Larry
Lawry
Len
Les Barton
Lowe
Mark Lewis
Marshall
Mazurke
McIntyre
McLachlan
McArdle
McNeill
Meehan
Meyrick Jones
Mico
Mike Sheill
Mike Turner
Mike Williams
NAF
Neil Bennett (NB)
Nick Baker
Nick Downes
Neil Dishington
Nick Hobart (Nick)
Pak
Pals
Parker
Pat
Paul Wood
Paulus
Pearsall
Philip Warner
Pidge
Reuben Beckett
R Besley

R Lowry
Ray Jones
Reading
RGJ
Rich
Richard Tomes
Robert Thompson
Roy Nixon
Roger Latham
Royston
RR
Russell
Sally Artz
Satz
Schwadron
Sewell
Siobhan McCooey
Smith
Spittle
Stan
Stan Eales
Steve Way
Stokoe
The Surreal McCoy
Tim Bales
Tony Husband
Waldorf
Warner
Waterhouse
Wilbur
Wilson
Wren
W Scott

'Your co-directors wish you a speedy recovery by a vote of 3 to 2'

HEINSTEIN
OF THE AIRWAVES

Bill Heine

Bill Heine

OXFORD AND CHERWELL VALLEY COLLEGE

056817

HEINSTEIN
OF THE AIRWAVES

Bill Heine

PUBLISHED BY

Chris Andrews Publications Ltd

Oxford & Cherwell Valley College
Library

Acc. No. O56817

Class: 914.2574 HEI

Location OX   Date 5/09

Published by:
Chris Andrews Publications Ltd
15 Curtis Yard
North Hinksey Lane
Oxford
OX2 0LX
Tel +44(0)1865 723404
Web: www.cap-ox.co.uk

ISBN 978-1905385-980

First published 2008
© Text: Bill Heine
© Pictures: Chris Andrews unless otherwise noted
© This design and production: Bill Heine and Chris Andrews
Design: Mike Brain

All rights reserved. No part of this publication may be
reproduced, stored in a retrieval system, or transmitted, in
any form or by any means, without prior permision of the
copyright holder. The right of Bill Heine as author of this work
have been asserted by him in acordance with the Copyright,
Designs, and Patents Act 1998

Every effort has been made to contact copyright holders
and check accuracy of inclusions. In the event of errors or
omissions the publishers will be happy to make corrections on
subsequent editions

Picture credits: Chris Andrews except for

Front Cover: Korky Paul,
Back cover and pps 2, 3, 7, 12, 16, 17, 34, 75, 78, 112,
129: *Oxford Mail*

John Henshall (p II)
Corbis (pp 6, 41)
Joanna Innes (p 84)
Marcello Capotosti (p 102)
Simon Farr (p 109)
Alun Jones (p 131)
Warner Bros (p 148)
Jon Davison (p 151)
Steve Archibald – stea@bigcatsightings.com (p153)
Joanna Dudderidge (p 166)

DEDICATION

This is dedicated to the rest of the team – Jane and Magnus who tore the book apart word by word at every opportunity, Harriet and Olivia who squirmed through it all on ring side seats, Peter, Anne and Ezra, a Greek chorus of quiet encouragement, if that's possible, and Beth who had her own, very definite, views ... about everything.

ACKNOWLEDGEMENTS

One person I never thought I would thank is my current boss, the Editor of BBC Oxford, Steve Taschini. At the beginning he dissed the book which gave me the determination to prove him wrong and write it. We battled all the way through until finally he helped shape and edit the text with a deft touch.

I've had a running fight with our local newspaper, the Oxford Mail, which considered me 'the opposition' for these past twenty years. I've taken them to the Press Complaints Commission, so I wasn't expecting to thank the current editor Simon O'Neill, but his generosity and help along with that of the picture editor, Jessica Mann, proved invaluable.

Some people are so anally retentive they can regurgitate every mistake you've ever made; but it is with unbegrudged gratitude that I thank my bouncers -- people who will toss around ideas with you -- Ted Dewan, Helen Kidd, Chris Oram, Abigail Uden and Tim Peach.

Joe Smyth was the sure footed guide who helped me wend my way past the 'angel of death'. *The Sunday Times* and the *Sunday Telegraph* kindly allowed me to reprint my articles from their pages.

'Straight' and 'narrow' are two words I don't like but when you string these together I hate them. A whole team tried to keep me on the straight and narrow – publisher Chris Andrews, editor Alex Antscherl, designer Mike Brain and lawyer John Simms.

Contents

Chapter 1

A Yank at Oxford

How to pole vault onto the airwaves with the tail of a shark.

The BBC sacked me three times one afternoon. Thames Valley Police blacklisted me for two years. A paedophile put out a contract on my life, and a pack of hunting hounds urinated over me during an outside broadcast – all part of the lie of the land for a BBC local radio presenter. But I wasn't local and I wasn't a presenter at the start, so how did a Yank at Oxford fly below the radar of the BBC Establishment and manage to stay on the air for twenty years?

This tale began with a shark . . . in my house. I have a shark's tail crashing through the roof, shattering the tiles. I bought this home in Oxford on 15 April 1986, the same day that US planes from nearby Upper Heyford airbase bombed Tripoli. That night I watched the TV news reports showing houses like mine in safe leafy streets with huge gaping holes in their roofs.

A few days later, on 26 April, the Chernobyl nuclear eruption spewed another kind of danger in the safe suburbs of Kiev.

April showers were disturbing roots that might produce strange fruit. It felt like the world was out of kilter and becoming curiouser and curiouser; anything could happen – from white rabbits wearing watch fobs to great white sharks leaping through the sky.

John Buckley, a sculptor with an eye on the zeitgeist, came to a house-warming and after four bottles of Veuve Clicquot we spent fifteen minutes bouncing ideas around. John produced the shark several months later on 9 August – the anniversary of the second atomic bomb dropping on the Japanese city of Nagasaki.

We wanted to ask a simple question. In our everyday lives, when we go about the business of cracking stone or sculpting it, how safe are we from the results of decisions by people in power? And we wanted to ask in a way that involved the public, caught them off guard and made them smile.

Of course it backfired. This 25-foot-long fibreglass work of art got me in deep water with my neighbours, the Oxford planning committee and every right-thinking person who wanted to stave off the disintegration of society and the onset of social chaos. This shark was a red flag to John Bull. It was also the trigger for my explosion onto the airwaves

For six years the headlines rolled off the press.

A FRIGHT ON THE TILES.

Shark could be a killer, say residents. The famous rooftop shark sculpture in Headington has been branded a menace – to road users.

SHARK TOURIST TRAP

– but the fish may have had its chips.

Oxford City Council railed against 'this blaggard', 'this victory for anarchy', 'this slap in the face for decent and respectable people'.

The battle went from the council to the courts to a public inquiry to the Cabinet. The Secretary of State for the Environment, Michael Heseltine, came to Oxford, walked up and down the Shark Street and

made the final decision. 'Into this archetypal urban setting crashed (almost literally) the shark. The contrast is deliberate . . . [but] an incongruous object can become accepted as a landmark after a time, becoming well known, even well loved in the process.'

The media, in love with conflict, emotion and character, pounced on the story and through the shark years I lived in a public goldfish bowl under intense scrutiny and questioning from BBC Radio Oxford. Finally the boss there took me to a long liquid lunch and asked me to come over to his side of the microphone. He used some marvellously madcap methods to persuade. 'This means you've made it, Bill. You'll be able to open supermarkets, shopping malls and earn lots of money, which is why we're going to pay you peanuts, but, hey, this is the beginning of something big.'

On Halloween 1988, the BBC sent me out over the airwaves on the lunchtime phone-in programme with a wing and a prayer, without any experience, training or parachute. It was pretty scary.

That was probably the last time the BBC ambushed someone in the street and made them overnight into a main sequence presenter in the daily schedule. Auntie Beeb did cover her back though. I got a one-paragraph letter that was the only 'contract' I had for the first five years. It said we would 'try this out for two or three months. Of course we have to point out you could be fired at any time because obviously we don't want to have someone on air who is a liability and you wouldn't want to be a burden to the BBC, would you?'

ENDANGERED SPECIES !

THE HEADINGTON SHARK

THE RECENT GALES MAY NOT HAVE DISLODGED THE HEADINGTON SHARK, BUT CITY BUREAUCRATS, BEHIND CLOSED DOORS, HAVE HATCHED PLANS TO DO SO.

The Court has ruled that Sharks on rooftops require planning permission and Mr Bill Heine, the sculpture's owner has complied with this edict. Meanwhile the Shark hunters in City Hall have pre-empted the coming Planning Committee meeting , by deciding, **without public consultation**, that the Shark must go. ! This meeting is scheduled for early March and action is required **NOW**.

The Shark has many friends; if you are one, you can help save this Oxford landmark. Make you views known in writting, or telephone;

The Shark is the inspiration of two men, Mr Bill Heine and sculptor John Buckley. It was conceived at the time the Americans bombed Tripoli via the UK and erected on Nagasaki Day 1986. For further information contact: S.O.S Committee, 21 New High St, Headington, Oxford.

Printed by Barbell Press. Recycled paper by E.S.P.

A.J.Walker Esq,
City Planning Officer,
Clarendon House,
52 Cornmarket Street,
Oxford OX1 3HD.
Telephone Oxford 252183.

Opposite. *The sculptor John Buckley and I with friends toasting the first precarious birthday of the shark. It still didn't have planning permission.*

Chapter 2

Is Local Provincial?
Does it pass the 'So What' test?

For a generation I've carried on a conversation with people in Oxfordshire about births, deaths, loves and hates. There have been couples that wooed and won each other over the airwaves, and people who lost each other. But does any of it reverberate in a wider world? Just how local is local radio? Well, sometimes not very – we occasionally travel as far away as Reading, a full forty miles.

In August 1996, Reading Borough Council hosted an exhibition about the diary of Anne Frank, which I visited and discussed on air. There really was not much to say about it. The story was a very personal and emotional one, giving a moving experience of a different time and place, unimaginable to some, distanced by time to all.

Then Hans from Reading rang the programme. He had a slight accent and explained he was originally from Holland. 'I remember those times very well – 1943-44. I was a teenager, thirteen or fourteen, and I worked on a farm outside but quite near to Amsterdam.

'Food was in short supply, but since my father grew grain, we were fortunate, we had enough. We had a good life and I was a strong lad. Many in the city, though, were hungry, so during the harvest we put by extra sacks to give to other people.

'My father sent me to Amsterdam on regular evening errands loaded with bags of corn, wheat and barley. It was not easy. The bags were heavy; we tied them to my back and chest under a cape. I walked all the way from the farm into the city to distribute them. It had to be early enough not to attract attention . . . not too late or I might be caught by the Nazis.

'I remember one night I pitched up with the last sacks at a house by one of the canals, and the owner quickly dragged me in saying I must stay the night because it was late, and if the Gestapo got me, that would destroy a lifeline to more people than I knew.

'He gave me something to eat and a bed, which was hidden away under the stairwell that led to the attic. It was a small space and uncomfortable, but I stayed there that night. At first light he woke me and said I must go immediately. Later the same day I found out that shortly after I left, the Gestapo raided the house, found the door and stairwell where I had been sleeping moments before, marched up to the attic and arrested the family of Anne Frank.'

Those war years provided other insights and experiences which illuminated small but personal chapters of that epic story.

One hot, lazy summer afternoon I was discussing on air the colours of the evening sky, a peaceful, whimsical enough subject until Eva rang. 'I remember …' (always those deceptively detonating words) 'One night the sky went red. I was working the late shift at a hospital in Coventry when the Luftwaffe flew over. The sound of the planes was blotted out by the bomb explosions. When the grey smoke broke, we could see the orange and red fires above.

'I was a nurse so I kept my eyes mostly on the ground. I can tell you exactly what happened when the bombs fell around us. We were almost opposite the Cathedral, and I saw what happened. People say Coventry Cathedral fell. I can tell you it didn't. I was there. I saw it. When the bomb hit, it didn't fall. It rose. The cathedral jumped in the air for a few heart beats, and then it came down.'

A different kind of bomb went out over the airwaves when John rang from a village in Buckinghamshire. He was a former Navy man who had served in the South Pacific in the Fifties. 'I was a young recruit happy to be sent to a kind of paradise called Christmas Island. The officers didn't tell us much, only that the Air Force was conducting an experiment and we were going to witness something pretty big.

'I remember the day well, 15 May 1957. It was very early in the morning. We had dug a trench and were told to stay down, turn to the north and close our eyes. On no account were we to look at the explosion. It was good advice. Even with my eyes closed the explosion created a white blast inside my head.'

'So you witnessed the first British atomic bomb test?'

'Yes, after a short time we were told it was safe to look; and we saw the mushroom cloud growing.'

'Did you have any protection?'

'No, they said we didn't need any because the winds mostly went east and the radioactive problem from the blast, we were told, was very minimal. It was the danger to our eyes from the flash that made it necessary to be in the trench, facing away from the blast which was thirty miles south of Christmas Island.

'Unfortunately there was some wind shift because of the blast, and we were outside in the trench when this happened. I didn't feel anything in particular, but I knew not everything went to plan. Well, my problem now is that I've been unwell, and my doctor recently told me I've got cancer. My mind keeps going over what happened then. I'm thinking about it, and I'm not exactly sure what to make of it.'

What remains of these stories from local people who didn't make the footnotes of history? At the time the airwaves were unavailable. Sometimes they had a tale to tell and maybe they didn't get it off their chest – the innocence of Hans, the anger of Eva and the fear of John. Then one day on local radio they have an opportunity and they grab it. So what? Does it mean anything? Does it matter? Does it change things? Probably not. But at least we now know; it adds to the sum of things, and they've unfurled their particular flag.

Chapter 3

Walter Mitty of Oxford

Some listeners may have incurable personality disorders.

'If you don't sort out my benefits by tomorrow, I'll come down there and knock the fucking shit out of you.' That was the message Phil left on the answer phone of his MP. His next phone call was to me.

'Hello, Bill. It's Phil . . . ' A familiar voice. We'd met several times on air.

'Oh, Phil, it's good to . . .'

'I'm just calling to say goodbye. Andrew Smith is a dead man. I'm going to kill him and then kill myself.' Click.

Andrew Smith was the Oxford East Labour MP and a cabinet member, the Secretary for Work and Pensions in Tony Blair's government.

I wasn't sure what to do. Phil had phoned my programme a few years ago from a telephone box in Didcot, South Oxfordshire, and threatened to kill himself. My producer kept talking to him off air while a researcher informed the police who traced the call and turned up at the phone kiosk to rescue Phil from himself. A few hours later Phil rang me back, very disappointed. 'Bill, how could you do that to me? You know I don't like the police. You know I'd never kill myself.'

I didn't know that, but I did remember he had been in court before on some serious charges and had ended up a patient for eleven years in Rampton, a high-security psychiatric hospital. Now this was not only a suicide threat, but also a threat to kill someone else. Was he serious?

I didn't think so, but as a loyal player for team BBC, I referred this up to the news editor. This BBC protocol is a way of covering your back, not going out on a limb by taking a decision on your own, and instead going for collective responsibility. But once I told the news editor, I crossed a line and lost the ability to call the shots and to call an end to this drama.

The BBC notified Thames Valley Police who sprang into action and scoured the country to find the potential killer of a cabinet member. The Secretary for Work and Pensions was alerted and his security increased. This was now an issue of national importance.

The police found Phil, with difficulty. He'd been sleeping rough. That was the cause of the death threat.

It turned out that Phil had been having a tough time, going in and out of treatment and hospitals, but he had finally got his life together. He was settled, clear-headed, out of trouble and in his own flat. He received benefits from the government of £165 per week and was spending a few pence less: Mr Micawber's idea of happiness.

But disaster struck. The Department for Work and Pensions made a mistake, which they later admitted, and cut his allowances by more than half, to £72. His life collapsed. Suddenly he couldn't pay the rent and didn't have enough to eat.

Phil made several complaints but to no avail, so he focused his anger on the Secretary of State for Work and Pensions, Andrew Smith. The Department said they would look into his entitlements but in the meantime Phil had to deal with the slings and arrows of what was becoming the ordinary life of a down-and-out. He was evicted and lived on the streets or in hostels, and all the other props of his life disappeared. Finally he left that threatening message on the answer phone of Andrew Smith.

The man behind this threat was about five feet tall, slightly overweight and yet frail-looking, with very thick glasses. His most developed muscles were probably his vocal chords; no one would describe him as 'lean and mean'.

He also had years of mental health problems. When Princess Diana rescued a tramp some years before from a pond near Buckingham Palace, Phil rang me to say he was that tramp. When Robert Maxwell was in the headlines, Phil emerged as a family friend. He also claimed to be connected with the al-Fayed family. At the age of forty-five Phil had a history of problems and illusions that would sit happily beside those of Walter Mitty.

The police officers in Oxfordshire who had to judge the credibility of this threat had known Phil over a few decades as a vulnerable person. The CID asked me to give a statement for the prosecution. At first I did not want to give one because I thought that he would end up in prison, but I was reassured by the CID officer that it would help him get treatment. On that condition I agreed. My statement formed the basis of the case for the prosecution and Phil pleaded guilty to threatening to kill a cabinet member. I attended court to hear the sentence.

In the pre-trial period he was interviewed by a psychiatrist who concluded that he had a paranoid personality disorder which cannot be treated. We also heard that neither the psychiatrist nor the police could find any evidence that he tried to carry out his death threat or his suicide threat. The psychiatric report concluded that in the light of his history and in the absence of serious risk factors, his risk to others was 'relatively low'.

The judge summed up that Phil had an untreatable mental illness and required support to keep out of trouble. In these circumstances what is a reasonable sentence, and what kind of support system should he have to help him get back on his feet?

The judge decided to send Phil to prison with an eighteen-month sentence.

What did this mean in practice? Phil's barrister mentioned in court that his client had been held in Bullingdon Prison on remand for over two months already and had been the subject of bullying. He was vulnerable, some would say not culpable, but most would agree he needed support.

Phil has written me many letters and phoned several times since, so I know his version of 'doing time'. He says he was bullied. Prisoners took his glasses and smashed them. When he could barely see, he was disoriented and then he was raped, repeatedly.

He was released from prison on licence. Then I received another letter, this time from Bedford Prison, saying, 'I've been out of prison twice since we last spoke, and each time it's failed because I've been let out with nowhere to go. No accommodation was found for me and no benefits sorted out either. I've not re-offended. The powers-that-be have just revoked my licence every time and returned me to prison through no fault of my own. No one wanted to take any responsibility for me.'

All this time his letters keep coming through to me with one main theme – 'Just a few lines to let you know how sorry I am and to apologise for all the trouble and stress that I caused you. I really am deeply sorry.'

Where is he now?

Chapter 4

The Run-up to the Race

Roger Bannister on life before he hit the tape.

One local story that ran and ran for over fifty years involved an Oxford graduate who cast himself in the role of an athletic Hamlet – to be or not to be the man who broke the four-minute mile.

The finish was an iconic moment when twenty-five-year-old Roger Bannister broke the tape at the University's Iffley Road track. Everyone knows about the race, and the rest is history. I had an opportunity to look at the run-up to that race, for local BBC listeners.

On the fiftieth anniversary of his victory, Sir Roger and I met up at the famous track for a couple of circuits, not running but not walking either. He's almost all legs and even in his golden years does not suffer slowpokes gladly.

During our trot down his track I asked him about his childhood. Was there a moment when he'd felt as if a finger had loomed up, tapped him on the shoulder and announced, 'You are a runner'?

He was philosophical. 'Our images and memories of childhood are often ill-formed; we can't say quite how old we were, or where we were when things happened. But I can undoubtedly remember being on a beach, probably at the age of four or five . . . sunshine, clouds scudding by, barefooted on the sand . . . and feeling suddenly alive to the desire to run. I was startled and started to run and I went on running just faster and faster; and then I probably lay down on the sand and laughed, exhausted. I can remember some experience like that.

'As I grew up through adolescence, this capacity to run without pain or discomfort became part of me and found its expression in running cross-country, running with friends for the sheer enjoyment of running across the countryside; and eventually this became a track event with more and more people watching and people concerned with stopwatches.'

Sir Roger Bannister and I looking to the past at Iffley Road track.

I could connect with some of that. I was a runner, of sorts. The half-mile was my race and I did hold a few records, which were soon enough smashed, but I obviously didn't have the dedication that he had so deftly glossed over. I asked Sir Roger if running had become an obsession for him.

He was emphatic on that one. 'I had to run at that stage in my life. It was a counterbalance to work and to the experience of growing up, in which we often have some difficulty finding out who we are, where we are going and what we want to achieve. We have both at the same time a sense of power and ability within us and yet also a sense of powerlessness. These two have to be fused in some kind of activity, it could be music or drama or writing. There can be any number of ways in which we find something in ourselves which we think is unusual, worth working on. It may not be remarkable and it may fizzle out, but it gives us something to occupy our minds until we start growing up.'

He was getting into a grey area here, the balance between the exuberance of power and the burden of powerlessness, and I asked him to explore further.

'I felt conscious that I was moving somewhere, but I didn't yet know where, although I intended to become a doctor. When I came up to Oxford at seventeen there were eight years of medicine and research ahead, so I looked for something else I could do as well. I think when you are young you feel you could do very many different things. Certainly my interests were very wide and they remained wide until, partly by chance, I discovered that I was still able to run, even in this seemingly adult Oxford world.

'At a time when there was austerity and a twenty-five pound travel allowance, I found I was able to travel almost anywhere in the world where there were tracks, and people who wanted to see me run and compete. You might say in a way it is an unimportant activity, but it certainly filled a gap in my life until I became a doctor.'

I wanted to understand that 'seemingly adult Oxford world'. He came up to Oxford in 1946, a fresher at Exeter College. That was a remarkable intake year because the dam broke after all those war years, and people who would have been at Oxford but went to war turned up at the university in their mid-twenties, many of them ready to compete in top-level sport. How did this seventeen-year-old cope?

'I went to find a place to run first of all, because I didn't really dare go down to the athletics track. I went to the Exeter College rugby ground and ran there with a friend. I remember the groundsman who had looked after Jack Lovelock, the great Oxford Rhodes scholar, Olympic 1500-metre winner in Berlin, the groundsman who watched after him – I don't think one could dignify it by saying he was Jack Lovelock's coach.'

Here I detected something akin to restrained disdain.

'He said to my companion, "I think you could run very well" and then he turned to me and said, "I don't really think you've got the physique for it." I suppose I was rather ungainly and was loping along. But I learned then that other people's opinions are not to be taken too seriously.'

The young Roger Bannister rose through the ranks of the athletics hierarchy to become president of the University Club. I asked him how he got on in that role.

'I had come from a fairly straightforward background; I hadn't come from a famous school. In Oxford at least ninety per cent of the students were ex-servicemen. So I was seventeen and they had won medals and been through battles and prisoner-of-war camps. They were very brave, and we from school didn't really know if we had been subjected to the same stresses, whether we would have reacted as well as they did. We would never know. All we could do was to try and do the best we could in the situation which then faced us.

'I found myself in an unusual role for an undergraduate. I suppose I was then eighteen and the youngest, perhaps, of the team. I naturally felt overawed.'

The first thing a new athletics club president does is set out his goals in a speech, so I asked if he was as good at speaking as at running.

'I realised that you have to keep cool and calm and have rehearsed what you want to do and say, but detach yourself in such a way that you don't become confused and muddled. I think that was the first time I learned that particular lesson. I suppose none of us finds it easy to speak in public but it slots into place as the years go by.'

I knew Sir Roger was a very private man, so how did he react to the pressures all those years ago? It was a seminal speech and after he fluffed it, he ripped up the sheets of paper and started all over again – this time speaking from the heart.

'What happened was that I knew what I wanted to do while I was president, and instead of thinking about my performance and their judgement of me as a maker of speeches, I connected with my ideas for changing the track – that was the first thing . . .'

So Oxford's track was not up to scratch. I asked him what was wrong with it.

'It had been built in 1890 and it was three laps to the mile. We ran the wrong way around it for some obscure reason, and there was an elm tree whose roots went through it. The unwary, usually our opponents from other universities, might catch their spikes in it; and if they entered or approached the area of the roots in the lead, by the time they passed the tree they certainly weren't leading. So I said we had to build a new track. We had to raise the money.'

'That's an amazing vision, some might say arrogant. Did your speech raise any eyebrows?'

'I think probably the audience had felt something like, "Well, we've elected this chap, is he really up to the job?" At first I think they may have begun to wonder – you know one is self-conscious of what effect one is creating – but then, when I started the speech all over again, they began to see that, yes, he does know what he wants to do; and he sounds as though he is going to be able to do it. He sounds as though he may be able to raise the money from the Rugby Club or from some other sources.

'In those days it was part of Oxford athletics, and I think still is, that Oxford undergraduates organise the sport. It is not dons or senior people. It's the president who arranges things. I said I would hire a professional coach. There had never been such a post but technical events required technical teaching. People thought running was straightforward and it had been left to the first string to teach the younger runners. That was the way it had worked.

'So all these changes, it seemed to me, had to happen at a time when we were in the first phase of austerity. It was the end of the war and people were wondering whether there could be growth and success in this country.'

A nineteen-year-old was telling people, mostly his betters and elders, they were going to have a new track. I asked how he pulled that one out of the hat.

'Well, there was a generation, if you like, in school terms, who were eight years older than me, who had been flying Hurricanes at the age of nineteen. They had been shot down and had performed acts of bravery in the armed forces, in the air, on the sea. So nineteen is an age at which you probably have high levels of competence although less confidence.

'With my secretary, who was a good friend, we went through the Yellow Pages and picked a constructor who came from Reading. We got £37,000 which came from the University Rugby Club. They were

'...and this is how you break the four minute mile.'

the only club that earned money because the annual match against Cambridge at Twickenham was a very big event immediately after the war. We had very good rugby players.

'The money from Twickenham went into the central athletic fund and when it came out again, I managed to persuade the bodies that controlled the money that it should flow in the direction of replacing our old athletics track which I said was a disgrace to the university.'

I wondered if there was any master plan at work here. 'Was that your idea – to get the track first and then focus on using it as the venue where one day you would break the four-minute mile?'

'It certainly wasn't as conscious as that. At the time I was president of the athletics club, I had won the mile race in successively quicker times over four years. But I think my time was only about four minutes seventeen seconds, so there was no prospect then of something like a sub-four-minute mile. Over eight years my times gradually dropped, and of course my objective then was to win the 1500-metres in the Helsinki Olympic Games in 1952. When I came in fourth place that Olympic failure made me try harder.'

But why did he come fourth at the Olympics? Could it be down to the fact that he chose very curious routes to run along, on and off track? 'You often did things on your own and in your own way. What is your view of having a coach?'

'Well, certainly one of the early coaches said to me: "I am the coach, you are the runner and I will tell you the running times when I think it is proper and useful for you to know them." There was this mystique of having an athlete who was an automaton, who was directly under the instruction of the coach, although not all relationships were like that. So in the early years I asked a number of coaches their opinions, but I never believed everything they said or did everything they thought I should do.

'To me, running was a sport in which control over your own destiny and style of training was part of the game. If you ran well or badly you had to find out why and it was a matter of trial and error. It wasn't a question of having special medical knowledge. It was this trial and error, which only you could feel from the effects of the training or degree of fatigue which would enable you to modify your training accordingly. So this seemed to me a perfectly logical way of conducting my training. Running is very simple. It can be reduced to terms of simple self-expression and effort.'

'Effort, yes,' I agreed but success requires a lot of little things. When he came to Oxford on that May day in 1954, it was rather blustery. I asked him what the weather was like exactly.

Sir Roger was almost all legs and I had to trot to keep up on our tour of his track.

'Well, I think 'blustery' is an understatement. There was a gale and there was a storm, and it looked like an early May day at the time of the equinox when the weather can't make up its mind. So I was very doubtful whether it was worth attempting, because to run in high winds means you have to run four seconds faster, at least, in order to break four minutes.

'I was very doubtful – until about half an hour before when I looked at the flag of St George on the church opposite the Iffley Road track and it seemed that the wind was slackening. I still say it was only fifty-fifty but I realised that if I didn't make the attempt then, when the conditions were just possible, I might never get another chance. I might never forgive myself; and I would have a long time to think about it afterwards.'

He said that with a decisiveness and a chiselled jaw which clearly indicated, to borrow an image from another sport, how far the archer had pulled the bow before this particular arrow hit the bull's eye.

Chapter 5

A Little Friendly Advice
The perks of broadcasting.

I'm often asked what are the perks of the job for BBC local radio presenters. What are those little 'leg ups' for the mouth behind the microphone, the preferment, the nod, the wink, the handshake, the advantage? It's a delicate subject and nobody talks about it much, with good reason – we don't want to admit that the cupboard of kudos is bare. I've been searching the airwaves for that trap door to opportunity during the last twenty years and it isn't there.

We do, however, have access to a wide group of people with influence and expertise, people at the top of their game who know the pitfalls, the roads not to take. Some of these people might be useful; they could come in handy to someone starting out on a journey. What's wrong with a little friendly advice from a professional? So I decided, shamelessly, to take advantage of one of these high fliers. This was probably as close to a perk as I was ever likely to get.

Well, he wasn't really one of your A-list authors. This tall, lanky, middle-aged, balding, former Oxford school teacher had published a few books and I'd interviewed him five or six times. Now he turned up at the BBC with a new book, the first of a trilogy. 'So why a trilogy?' I asked.

'Lots of reasons,' he replied, 'mostly commercial and strategic. One big thick book might put people off and the publishers reckon if readers like the first book we'll get a second and third bite of the cherry.' I liked the gutsy honesty as well as the book.

I was trying to write a book myself – the story of the shark in my roof. I'd just finished the first chapter and wanted to bounce it off someone. Why not this particular high-flier who had winged his way into the web of his BBC local radio presenter? I was getting a second opinion; nothing unethical in that.

I chose to tell the shark story through the eyes of – the shark, naturally enough. So I had this fibreglass sculpture diving head first through my roof narrating the story of how she got stuck there and what she thought of the person who made her, the person who invited her into his roof and the authorities who were out to kill her. It was a cross between a science fiction morality play and a surreal murder mystery told from the point of view of a great white shark who was not a happy bunny. She was an angry animal grinding what few teeth she had left at the cruelty and insensitivity of the sculptor, the stupidity of the owner and the arrogance of the authorities. She had it in for everyone. I thought it was a recipe for such success that I would approach a Broadway producer and maybe turn it into a musical, 'Springtime Will Bite Back'.

I sent it off to my author friend with high hopes. The reply that came whizzing back hit me in the jaws. It was revealing, not so much about my aspirations but about his.

Dear Bill,

I'm certain there's a good book to be written about the shark, but I don't think this is it.

You need to decide what the story is going to be. Is it 'Lone eccentric fights philistine bureaucracy and wins', or is it 'It's a funny world', or is it 'Art, Politics, and the Media: A Sociology of Culture', or is it 'Heroic individual redefines Post-Modernism for the masses'? Whatever line you take doesn't in itself matter, but they each need to be structured differently and told in a different tone.

If I were you I'd go for the human angle. The story's about you, actually. And it comes alive here when we hear the voices of the neighbours; you're good at that. Don't have the shark speak at all. Tell your story in your own voice. And don't write it like a novel. Start on the morning of the shark's arrival; go back to what led you to put it up, including as much of your colourful past as is relevant and printable; and then move forward through all the comic posturing of the council and so forth (plenty of comedy there, as long as you do it straight) to the final triumph.

In short: when you've got a good story (and you have, in spades) tell it as straight as you can. Don't fuck about with different angles and funny voices. I can see (a) a successful book, which will be both popular because it's a cracking yarn and critically praised because it shines a particular and unusual light on a corner of English social history; (b) a TV film which will clean up at BAFTA; (c) appearances on The Late Show, Arena, Question Time – and then the world, as Arthur Daley used to say, is your lobster, my son.

But do it straight. That's my advice.

All the best,

Yours,

Philip Pullman

Some reply – some perk. That cured me of ever wanting to take advantage of my 'position' again. From now on I was going to do this radio gig straight.

Chapter 6

Shots in the Neck

The BBC can be a very good gunslinger.

The corridors of the BBC are littered with the bleached bones of former presenters who hung on too long; others just scuttle away to the bushes to lick their wounds and die. It's a career that always ends in tears. During one afternoon Auntie Beeb shot me in the neck three times. I'm not exactly sure why – probably something like 'bringing the BBC into disrepute', 'using an obscene gesture on radio' and 'being too creative for your own good'.

This little attack happened in 1991 after the first Gulf War and before the public debate on post-traumatic stress disorder and the Gulf War syndrome. Former soldiers started ringing me to air their grievances about their training, the lack of equipment, the cocktail of vaccinations, the destruction and deaths they witnessed and the difficulty of coming home to civvie street. Some were distressed; some sounded like they were in shock. So I asked if they had had any counselling.

That simple question opened the floodgates for a torrent of abuse aimed at me. 'Counselling is the modern disease. If people have the slightest difficulty they run to the psychologist – doesn't matter what it is: marriage, money, the military. Don't take responsibility for it and sort it. Find some crutch of a counsellor, spend a lot of time and money going around in circles and clichés, and you'll come out of it none the wiser. It's time this generation stood on it's own two feet. We did.'

This led to a huge debate on counselling. Everyone had an opinion, but few had any experience. The more the 'anti' were full of certainty and passionate intensity, the less they knew. So I decided to arrange a counselling session on air. It would not be a typical two-minute sound bite, but a full twenty-minute session of something that was as close to the real thing as we could get; and then we would discuss it on air with listeners.

I invited Nick, a psychologist at the local university, to give a live demonstration and he came up with a plan that fitted well into the medium of radio by including the use of sound, not just words. On the day, he turned up with an actress who would play his 'client' in the counselling session. We started out with a background statement from me on air about the debate and the need for more information. Here was a way into the process of counselling, a live demonstration with a psychologist and an actress playing his client. 'Please don't misunderstand. This is a radio broadcast, not the real thing. This is not a psychological War of the Worlds, so don't jump to conclusions or out the window.' And besides we were dealing with the inner world of a person, so how could anyone be frightened or offended by that? We were on safe ground.

Nick and his client 'Natasha' began. They were sitting at a table in the studio with two microphones and two newspapers, the Guardian and the Daily Mail, as it happens. Natasha was distressed and began talking about problems with her boyfriend; every time she gave an example of his behaviour that she hated, she emphasized this by hitting her knee. Eventually the audience heard the sound of someone pummelling herself.

'What are you doing?'

'Nothing.'

'With your hand?'

'Nothing.'

'You're hitting yourself.'

'No . . . I . . . am . . . not!' Each word was followed by a direct hit.

'Why are you doing that?'

They danced around this for a few minutes until Natasha shouted, 'I hate him. I just hate him.'

'Who?'

'Greg.'

'Your boyfriend's name is Charlie.'

'My father . . . I hate my father. He wasn't there when we needed him, when I was growing up. He walked out on us, on my mother and me. I was seven. I loved him and he just simply closed the door one day and never came back. How could he do that to me?'

Nick and Natasha talked through this until Natasha had no more words and retreated into primitive moans, grunts and groans: Ahaaa . . . ohahoh . . . uhaaah.

Nick went with this and instead of continuing to talk he followed her into sound. The result was a soprano 'ahhhhah' followed by a baritone 'ooohah' in syncopated rhythm. Then she grabbed the newspaper and starting ripping out the pages. Nick shouted, 'Yes, yes, yes' and they both clawed and scrunched the pages in time to the groans. They had moved from a conversation into a physical dialogue of sounds and raw emotion in less than one minute. The timing was impeccable – totally wrong.

The managing editor of BBC Radio Oxford had just returned to the station from a liquid lunch and made his way up to the second-floor loo. Whatever he was doing there soon became of secondary importance. After one minute of listening to passionate intensity over the loudspeakers in the loo he was full of certainty that this filth must be stopped. He ran into the office with his trousers undone and roared out something that, when cleaned up, translates roughly into, 'Bring me the head of William Randolph Heine.'

His henchmen started circling the studio. I could see shadows and then men in black with shiny shoes and bulging packets in the pockets. They pointed at me and shouted at my producer. It is possible to see blood drain from a face.

Meanwhile, back on the airwaves, the high-quality 'ohhah! – oh my god! – yes, yes, yes!' had stopped naturally and we were having a discussion of what counselling is all about, which was the purpose of the exercise. Then the verbal shots rang out in my earphone.

Nick (live on air) – 'What people say may not indicate exactly what they mean . . .'

Henchman (simultaneously in my earphone off air) –
'HEINE, YOU'RE FIRED. GET THIS CRAP OFF THE AIR
NOW. DID YOU HEAR ME? YOU'RE FOR THE HIGH
JUMP. NOW!!!'

Nick (on air) – '. . . and it's important to give people time and space to say what they mean. Every word is important.'

Henchman (off air) –
'YOU'RE DEAD MEAT. I'LL COME IN THERE AND KICK
YOUR ARSE OFF THE AIRWAVES IN TWO SECONDS,
AND AFTER THIS STUNT YOU'LL NEVER CRAWL
BACK ON.'

Nick (on air) – 'The whole point is to listen to what people have to say and find out what they mean.'

Henchman (off air) –

'THAT'S IT. I'M COMING IN AND I DON'T CARE
WHERE THE SHIT HITS.'

They didn't come in and like most henchmen they didn't have the courage of their boss's conviction. This bit of slippage allowed me to finish the programme and fight my own corner later with the head honcho and talk my way out of the guillotine.

He did give commands, three times, that all smiles should stop, but eventually settled down and accepted three apologies. So no bleached bones or bushes for me, yet; but at this point who needed counselling?

Chapter 7

Urban Terrorism

An Oxford neighbourhood under siege.

Oxford is not so much one city as many communities. Some are full of people with initials – MPs, the DG of the BBC, possibly even the KGB – who usually send their children to expensive local private schools and live in the leafy lanes of Dragonland, laughingly referred to by de Sade as Summertown. They mostly have money, high cheekbones and instant access to the media. Others suffer in silence. Wood Farm is one area with a lot of people suffering. But this silent minority in Oxford found its voice to fight fear, intimidation and violence using the airwaves.

The fight started with a single anonymous e-mail to me asking for help and snowballed into a debate that pulled in television, the press and even someone with initials, the PM. Entitled 'Under Siege', this email lit the torch.

> Bill, I'm writing to you in despair. There is a gang of vicious nasty thugs terrorising shopkeepers, shoppers and anyone else who happens to cross their path in the vicinity of the Atkyns Road shops on the Wood Farm estate. This has been going on for years and the police and authorities appear unable to put a stop to it.
>
> Recently one man has been driven from his home and people pelted with stones. Others do not go to their local shops for fear of intimidation and violence. Buses have been hit with water bombs and other missiles. The bus stop is regularly vandalised. The shops have had to install very expensive security grilles after repeated vandalism, and now we have been told the Co-op is to close as a result of the trouble. This is devastating to the many elderly and disabled for whom the local Co-op shop is a lifeline.

We have had to endure this urban terrorism for far too long, but with the police and Oxford City Council seemingly unable to have significant impact, it all looks like continuing until the community is destroyed.

PS You will understand after the content of what I have written that I wish to hide my identity and I will not come on air.

We rang the Oxford, Swindon and Gloucester Co-operative for a statement on whether they were planning to close their store in Wood Farm, and they were quite open: 'We share the concerns of local residents and our own store team face abuse and threatening behaviour on a daily basis. We would like to see long-term action to protect residents and traders alike. As a Co-op we have a social responsibility to support estates such as Wood Farm. However, for the safety and well-being of our staff, we are reviewing whether we have a long-term future in this area.'

After I read the e-mails on air, there was a pause in the programme as if people were adjusting their radio sets or their take on reality: 'We live in Oxford. We know what happens here. People aren't under siege. This can't be true.' Then came the cloudburst and roaring thunder of residents' fears and tales of intimidation, about their daily lives being turned upside down, turned into torture. The people who rang the programme did not want to use their names on air, but they all wanted to tell their stories.

Anonymous caller 10: 'I live in the tower block and there are three individuals in here who are being abused all the time. Two days ago I was stood outside the tower block talking to these people and the gang appeared. Two seconds later we were being pelted with stones and bricks and I was hit by a two-penny piece, which I picked up and put in my pocket. They have caused thousands of pounds of damage here. They even put the lifts out of action in the tower block, and we have fourteen floors here. This has been going on for six months, since before Christmas. The police gave us a "unique reference number". So five times I've called about this URN and five times I've had no response from the police.'

Anonymous caller 23: 'The youths actually broke into the surgery two times in one week. It wasn't a case of breaking in and nicking anything. It was pure wanton vandalism. They didn't just break in, they urinated everywhere and put graffiti all over. After that the police issued a crime number but did not even come out to discuss the matter. They didn't put in an appearance. There are so many decent, law-abiding people living on this estate, and they are worried about not only their own safety but what will happen to their services. What will they do when they lose their surgery?'

Anonymous caller 29: 'I'm in my thirties with two young children and lived here since I was born basically. I bought my property from the council to get on the ladder and now I want to sell it. The estate agent keeps coming back to me for the last nine months saying people love the property, it's beautifully presented; but they just don't want to live in the area. I grew up here as a little girl, and it was lovely. My mum lives here and she's elderly and now she wouldn't dream of going to the shops after four in the afternoon. I wouldn't want to tackle the gang and I'm young and fit. There is an undercurrent of fear here. The shops are a "no go" area in the evening. We don't deserve to feel like prisoners in our own homes.'

This saga went on for four days. Anonymous caller 35: 'After your programme yesterday we're all very grateful. At least today we had cameras, television, newspapers and police around. We feel very sorry for the shopkeepers and the chip-shop owners who feel particularly victimised. The people who run it call one of the councillors to escort them home at night. I believe their lease has been devalued and now they can't even sell up and get away from the problem. This is terrible. And the Co-op, it was originally set up to help out working-class populations and they don't like to pull out of areas like Wood Farm. I can tell you when the staff say they get threats and abuse daily, it is true. Everyone here, we're all afraid. Last night after your programme, for the first time I felt, "Hallelujah." I'm sixty-one and now I thought I can go out to the shops for a bottle of milk. They were all out there but for some reason I could walk among them without the usual shouts and abuse. Just two days ago I was pelted with stones, bottles and cans. They shouted "grass" at me because I talked to the police. We're used to getting water cannons in our gardens, believe me that's nothing. It's chicken feed.'

Anonymous caller 60: 'I live in Wood Farm and I don't think people realise what a loss it would be for the community if the Co-op were to go. We've been over there in the evening just before closing and the staff have been locked in with a piece of wood between the handles of the shop door. These kids are not thinking of anyone else's welfare. The youths had barricaded the staff in so they could not get out.

'This is great how all this has happened, how everyone has reacted to the programme because we are all fed up with it. The fact that we're all going anonymous explains how we all feel.'

But one person didn't mind giving me his name, Sidney: 'I'm disgusted and ashamed of all this, but there's not much we can do if the council won't help us. Joyriding, kiddies giving people a boot when they go to the shops, piddling on the landing of the tower block. They are using the place as a toilet; it's downright disgusting. If I go round the corner they shout at me, "You nonce, you nonce." I'm no nonce. I have to use a wheelchair when I go outside. I was taking my little dog for a walk one night. There are flats above the shops, and there were nine of the gang shouting at me from the balcony, "You nonce, you nonce." So I turned the wheelchair around, put on the brakes and looked at them and told them, "Come down here and say that." And they wouldn't come down, nine of them against one old cripple, eh! You know they never had the guts to come down.'

Every part of BBC Oxford, not only radio but television and the web pages too, ran with the story. These stories stunned the police, the press and the public. The media descended on the area and Wood Farm went in at number one that week on the agenda of Oxford City Council and Thames Valley Police whom we invited to respond to the callers. The police claimed they were too busy with other media pressures for interviews, which is the answer to one e-mail question I received from Chris the following day:

To the casual listener it sounds as if the very fabric of society is starting to fall apart for the poor souls living at Wood Farm. I find it astounding that the police have not accepted the BBC's invitation to comment on the situation. I'm sure it cannot be the case, but to someone like myself with no first-hand knowledge of the situation at all, it sounds like the police have just given up on the place and are expending their resources elsewhere. Did the police give any reason at all for not participating in the phone-in? If not, why not?

The debate sent ripples that lapped at the front door of 10 Downing Street. Two weeks later I interviewed Tony Blair and asked him three times before I got any focused answer about how such a thing as the Wood Farm failure could happen and the Prime Minister finally promised: 'I'll look into the problem of Wood Farm myself.'

What's changed? Well, people's sense of value and power and hope has changed. The idea that we-will-be-listened-to has taken hold. There has been regular, sustained high-profile policing, media monitoring and political strategy to remove the gang leaders and disperse the members. The leader was served with an Anti-Social Behaviour Order, banned from the area and finally landed in prison.

Things are different. Wood Farm is changing because the residents decided that the first step is to describe things using the airwaves so the events can't be ignored, to blow the whistle – and then they can change things, slowly.

Chapter 8

A Close Call

Blood on the microphone when a charity stunt goes wrong.

A BBC local radio presenter does not have a dangerous job, but it can be unpredictable, like the day I was hit in the jaw, held in a headlock, stripped naked and stuffed into a straitjacket.

Madness grips the BBC each year on Children In Need day. Staff will do anything this side of legal to raise money for charity . . . most staff. I wasn't interested, didn't want to dress up in old torn fishnet stockings and corsets and pretend to be having fun. So my cohorts at the BBC decided to redraw some legal lines and push me over the edge − into villainy.

I was presenting the lunchtime phone-in programme one year during Children in Need with my guest James Elles, a Member of the European Parliament for Oxfordshire, when the studio door banged open to reveal the Oxford Superintendent of Police and two photogenic women Police Constables. I was somewhat surprised but decided to ignore them until they arrested me on air. The top cop read out the indictment − for treason − under a centuries old Act of Parliament. 'You stand accused of attacking people in authority, undermining their power and position and exposing them to ridicule.'

Well, how could I argue with that one? Still I tried, until the police handcuffed and gagged me but not before I appealed to my MEP to step in. James Elles was ashen and then most indignant and promised to follow us to the police station and advised me 'not to say anything . . . more'.

The police put me in the back of the local Black Maria, turned on the blue lights, took me to the cop shop and booked me for treason. It was the second time in my life I had ever been finger-printed. This lot did it in a very messy manner. They cleaned up the excess ink and dumped me in a cell. If you've ever been to a pub loo that was designed to be hosed down as easily as possible after a heavy night you will have some idea of the décor.

I stretched out on the metal bunk of a bed, perchance to dream, when who should appear on the other side of the bars but my biggest nightmare and nemesis, someone in a position of power whom I had exposed to ridicule: the chairman of the Oxford City Council Planning Committee who was then trying to harpoon the shark in my roof. We were locked in a battle of wits over the rights and wrongs of the shark, and now that I was locked up he came down to turn the screw. The conversation went generally along these lines:

Chairman – 'The game is finally up. They've got you where you belong and I hope they throw away the key.'

Prisoner – 'That's a cliché. To which game are you referring?'

Chairman – 'You've been one of the biggest pains in the arse this city has ever seen, putting up that shark and then claiming it's a work of art. And you're always pointing the finger, criticising other people, making their lives hell, causing damage. You don't stop to think what effect you have on other people, do you? All you want is another headline. Well, now you're going to get headlines, the kind you deserve – big, bold and bad. You've been a bastard to the people who are doing their best to run this city and now at long last they have the chance to be one big bastard to you.'

Just what I wanted to hear. After an hour of this mental abuse, not to say torture, the police transferred me, under guard, to the Oxford Prison. The turreted stone walls, barbed wire and frosted cathedral-style wooden doors concealed a set of Victorian rabbit warrens within. I was escorted past the graveyard (yup, that's where they buried people that they hanged) to 'reception', where my clothes were exchanged for a prison uniform and I was examined – all orifices.

By this time I was so fed up I asked to see the doctor. He explained this was all routine, apparently everything in prison is 'routine'. I said I wanted my lawyer, my MEP and I wanted out. Since he wasn't responding, I upped the ante and raised my voice several decibels. He responded with a hypodermic.

I was 'saved' by a posse of, I think, five prison guards. Their leader, a southpaw, lashed out and went for my head; two grabbed my arms and two on my legs. I didn't touch the ground. They have techniques to control you involving the arms and shoulders; they dragged me kicking and screaming out of the room. The screams were all recorded by the BBC and when I heard them later they sounded serious. They were.

The posse dragged me down some narrow, twisting, dark Kafkaesque corridors in this rabbit warren when they suddenly stopped, ripped off my clothes (all the buttons on my shirt popped), threaded my arms though the sleeves of a white, now fashionable, wraparound and literally

Rebel Bill goes to jail

£¼m cash response to appeal

RADIO Oxford presenter Mr Bill Heine was arrested shortly before the end of his radio show yesterday.

He was charged with sedition, questioned at Oxford's St Aldate's Police Station and later detained at Oxford Prison.

But fans of "shark man" Bill's lunchtime chat show need not worry — the arrest was in aid of the BBC's Children in Need appeal.

And the Oxford Star columnist was released after listeners responded to Radio Oxford's plea for cash.

The warm-hearted response in Oxfordshire may have raised more than £¼m for the Children in Need appeal.

The total so far for the Radio Oxford area, which also includes parts of West Buckinghamshire, stands at £234,549.

But organisers say the figure will rise as the national total soars over the £20m mark.

● Picture: DAVE FLEMING

Bill Heine is handcuffed by WPCs Amanda Boocock and Karen Thacker

Two photogenic WPCs man handling me.

threw me into a padded cell (blue as I recall): the punishment block. The door slammed shut and then there was no sound. It was totally quiet in the isolation block of course, except for the heart beats, very very loud, the light creating some white noise and the drip-drip-drip of the sweat that I hadn't noticed during the 'action sequence.' I squirmed in my straitjacket to no avail and that was it.

If this was a BBC Children in Need stunt something had gone horribly wrong. It was too near the bone – the shoulder bone; I heard mine crack. Something that started out as a possible prank was now not funny.

After several hundred heart beats – you actually start counting them – the door opened and I could hear the applause and the comments – 'Well done, very convincing, you could have fooled us all with those screams' – and they were addressing me, trussed up, exhausted and almost ready to be exhumed.

The Children in Need charity made a lot of money out of this. They taped the whole thing, played it out on air and gave listeners to BBC Radio Oxford the option to donate money to keep me in prison or to let me out. The listeners were very jolly and pretty evenly divided about where I should spend the night. It was a close call, but I slept in my own bed, thanks.

A happier exit . . .

Chapter 9

'Would You Like to see my Gun?'
The police know how to bite back

'You stitched me up' is one of those pulp-fiction phrases that criminals hiss at cops in B-movies. In live BBC local radio programmes that sort of thing just doesn't happen; we're all too polite and too public. This time when the microphones went dead, so did the atmosphere in the studio. A policeman leapt out of his seat, grabbed me by the collar and spat that phrase right in my face with a staccato rhythm – 'You – stitched – me – up.'

The subject for debate was guns – should we follow the American police model and arm the British bobbies on the beat? I wanted a balanced discussion, so I invited three people with different perspectives. For an overview an expert from ACPO, the Association of Chief Police Officers, was on the telephone; and so was a person with an unfettered view, a retired policeman. The officer in charge of firearms for Thames Valley Police provided the local view in the studio.

The Inspector arrived early in reception at the station. Our receptionist, Sandy, greeted him with her usual double entendre – 'Is that a suitcase you're carrying or are you just pleased to see me?' He sank into the large, comfortable, leather sofa with a suitcase that turned out to be full of firearms. There was some banter between the two that ended with the policeman asking Sandy if she would like to see his guns. Sandy got up from her desk and walked over to the sofa and the Inspector got out his equipment to show her. She expressed surprise and amazement. They were interrupted after a few minutes when my producer buzzed through and invited the policeman into the studio for the interview.

During the news we had a few moments to talk off-air. He walked around the room the way a prize-fighter would move around the ring during the big match. He was either very confident or he was skittery. And he wanted to find out if I could roll with the punches. 'I've brought a few guns with me . . . some real ones and some fakes. I thought that would be helpful. If all police were armed, what would a constable do when confronted with someone holding a fake that looked just like the real McCoy? It's not easy to tell them apart. I'll test you on air.'

The debate eventually focused on fake versus real and the dangers this presented for both the cops and the criminals. The local police officer got out some weapons in the studio, placed them on the desk and asked me to pick out the fakes. Of course, not knowing one end of a gun from the other very well, I got it all wrong; but he had made his point and it was a valid one.

When the question of safety came up, the head of firearms at Thames Valley Police had several suggestions and spoke eloquently about the responsibility police officers had to control guns and ammunition. He was broadcasting about the need to be both vigilant and safe – 'whenever police officers carry a gun they have to be in full control of it at all times' – when I heard a click off-air in my earphones and then a voice. 'Bill, I'm in the next studio. Look at me.' It was the voice of Mark, our breakfast-show presenter. He was standing there, feet apart, arms straight out in front of him holding a gun, aimed at me through the window that divided his studio from mine. 'We found this on the sofa in reception,' he said in my earphone, 'and we think it belongs to your guest.'

The gun was discovered, I later learned, by the local postman who delivered the mail to Sandy in reception, had a chat with her, as apparently everybody does, and then started to leave until he got as far as the sofa. He stopped abruptly and asked Sandy if she knew there was a gun lying on the leather seat. Sandy took it all in her stride, told the postman not to worry and picked up a copy of the Radio Times, opened it to the centrefold and laid it gently over the gun.

Sandy pondered this gun that was unsafely out of sight. She wasn't exactly sure of the correct protocol; this was, after all, slightly new territory. Mark arrived in reception back from breakfast and full of beans. He reassured Sandy that he would handle it, picked up the gun, brought it into his studio and aimed it at me.

I was looking down the barrel of a pistol and listening to a policeman give a speech about gun safety. The question was – how to play it? Should I ignore the information I've had about the gun on the sofa? Should I decide on balance that courtesy to my guest and diplomacy and deference to the police must take priority? How would I react if this were a gunsmith in the studio with me or a marksman from a gun club or a collector of firearms? Did I have a responsibility to the listeners to tell it like it is? What were my principles; where did I stand? Sometimes you have to cut the cards and deal, on your own, because there is no time or opportunity for the luxury of consultation.

The officer in charge of firearms for Thames Valley Police finished speaking and I agreed with him it was very important to keep track of firearms. 'So,' I said 'you've brought various guns here to the BBC. Let's do an audit. How many guns did you bring into the building?'

Policeman – 'Six.'

Presenter – 'Yes, and could you tell me exactly where they are?'

Policeman – 'Well, I have three on the table in front of me as you can see, and um . . . two still in the suitcase.'

Presenter – 'Two? Are you sure?'

Policeman – 'Yes, two.'

Presenter – 'And you came in with six?'

Policeman –'Yes, well . . .'

Presenter – 'We found a gun in our reception area lying on the sofa, and our breakfast programme presenter is bringing it into this studio now. Can you identify it?'

Policeman – Silence. 'Yes, yes, it's one of mine. Thanks.'

Sometimes the airwaves go silent; you can, with a sixth sense, feel that the people listening are not talking, not moving for a moment. Then everything goes back to what some would call normal. We were all courteous, considerate and correct . . . until the end of the programme. That's when the police officer in charge of firearms at Thames Valley Police almost went ballistic. The only thing that stopped him was my producer walking in and congratulating us on a 'most amazing look at the pressures and priorities of the police'.

The officer left the building in a huff, but what legacy did the programme leave?

The police response time was incredibly fast. On the Saturday after the programme some staff from the police were scheduled to play football with a BBC Radio Oxford team. That match was cancelled immediately.

Thames Valley Police also refused to supply traffic and travel information to the whole station; so we did not get any help from the police on road traffic accidents, slow-moving vehicles, road closures, floods, spillages and motorway problems. That went on for some time until the BBC management team brokered a deal to get past this problem.

No one from Thames Valley Police would appear on my programme for two years. We couldn't get past the press office. As soon as my name was mentioned an icy chill filled the telephone line. My BBC editor even suggested I invite key people from the police to lunch and eat humble pie in front of them, a suggestion that I didn't find appetising.

I think the question at the heart of this episode was about impartiality. I played it straight down the middle; and I knew, as I was doing it, that I might get hit. I just didn't realise how many other people would get hit as well, how much of a problem my decision would cause my colleagues at the time. They are still divided over this one with accusations that 'it wasn't so serious . . . you hurt a lot of people . . . next time weigh the damage against the benefit.' Even at Thames Valley Police there is an old guard which harbours hatred on the grounds that 'if one policeman gets hit we all bleed'.

On some level broadcasting is not about debate and arguments, even on a current affairs programme like mine, even on the Today programme. It's about feeling, passion and emotion, which can be far more powerful than logic. All of a sudden radio can become alive in a new way, not because of a sequence of events or words, but because of a shift in perception, a click in the emotional landscape that you replay and replay but can't delete from your mind's system. Something has happened and it won't go away. It's emotional and it's got you, and some emotional wounds just don't heal.

Chapter 10

Bob and Betty
The Maxwells and the legacy they left Oxford.

Oxford has several characters who are large in life, but one in particular shrank and shrivelled in death – Robert Maxwell, boss of a publishing empire with thousands of employees, tycoon of the Mirror newspaper and saviour of the Oxford United football team, who took them to the top of the national game. When he disappeared from his yacht, the Lady Ghislaine, off the Canary Islands in 1991, Oxford, England and the world were spellbound. What happened? Was he pushed or did he jump?

The picture of this economic Dorian Gray quickly turned ugly. He had funded a lavish lifestyle and buoyed up his failing business interests by plundering the pension schemes of his employees. Many in Oxford who worked for this man on modest wages would now have little or no pension.

There was an outcry. People rang my programme and broke down in tears of disbelief and despair. Twins Cynthia and Sylvia had worked their whole lives in the printing business, mostly for Robert Maxwell. They were due to retire, but at eleven o'clock one morning a man with a clipboard walked into their workshop and told them not to return after lunch. That was it – no goodbye, no thanks and no pension.

Cynthia and Sylvia lived in a state of shock for months, walking around the streets of Oxford holding hands, not eating much, sitting in cold rooms without heat, draped in blankets. They lost more than money. Sylvia lost her health. Several times I met Cynthia pushing her twin in a wheelchair around Carfax, the centre of Oxford. After a short spell Sylvia died of cancer.

This was the Oxford that Robert Maxwell's widow, Betty, was entering when she joined me on air. Betty Maxwell had returned to her native France after the explosive end of the empire and was back in Oxford to promote her book, *A Mind of my Own: My Life with Robert Maxwell*. She had to have known the score: she was stepping into a minefield and I was not going to lead her through it.

I had never met Betty Maxwell before, although mutual friends had told me how she could be charming, disarming and forceful. My only contact with the family was with Ian, one of the sons, whom I met while he was a student at Oxford. When a local newspaper wrote an article about me that was not just biased, but pretty crude and rude, Ian gave me his father's telephone number so I could get some advice on how to deal with this.

The number turned out to be a hotline direct to Robert Maxwell's desk and the man himself answered. He knew the newspaper and the reporter. She had also written a knocking article about him and he 'slapped a writ with a hefty price tag on their desk with an immediate deadline. They caved in. It's the best approach – and I hope that bitch gets her left tit caught in a wringer.' Before I had time to comment he rang off.

So now I was going to meet 'the other half'. Who was this woman who lived with such a man? I had a mental image. I was prepared for almost everything but the surprises. Her voice was strangely . . . sexy. The French accent made her already rounded vowels positively curvaceous. She must have been in her seventies and yet here was a husky, frisky French fille talking about how she first met the love of her life, Robert Maxwell.

'He was very charismatic. He made great promises. He was, in a way, fulfilling a dream . . . the dream that a young, romantic, rather naïve girl could have had in my generation. He was promising for me a world that was only a world in my dreams, and to some extent he did make it come true.'

But then she would say that wouldn't she – painting a picture of herself as inexperienced, in love and innocent, caught in a time warp and in the arms of a megalomaniac? I wasn't convinced about the dream world and asked her if it was also a nightmare world.

'Well, unfortunately, yes, it wasn't all smooth sailing. He was a very demanding, a very possessive person. It was difficult, really, to be everything he wanted me to be. He wanted so much. He demanded all the love that I could give him. I suppose he had been bereft of the love of his own family, so that I was to be everything for him. I was his love, his lover, his wife, his mother . . . all that was wrapped into one.'

I could have explored that, but I decided to shift the conversation

Robert and Elisabeth Maxwell living the high life, but who picked up the tab?

to a different level. I asked her if she was damaged by her relationship with Robert Maxwell.

'No. I can't really say that because by the time I realised this dual personality he had, I was very much stronger. Far from being damaged, I think for a large part of my life, he made me a better person. He demanded from me things that I did not know I possessed. He stretched me. I gave the best that I had to please him and to please others through him, to help others through him; and I owe him that. I am a better and a stronger person because of him, so that was a gain not a loss.'

She was answering my questions directly and in a considered way, so I asked about Maxwell as a damaged person himself. During their life together she said he had changed quite radically; I wanted to know why she thought that happened.

'Well, I think towards the end of his life he was an immensely sick man. He was sick physically...'

I wasn't going to let it stop there. Yes, I agreed, he was sick physically, but what about morally?

'Yes, I think that is another story. Sometimes one wonders how anybody who has gone through the war, through the Holocaust in the way he did ... lost everyone around him ... can ever be normal. I mean the miracle is that so many of those that survived such traumas can operate fairly logically. I think he was himself very much damaged by what happened to him in his youth.'

That wasn't a clear picture of the man, so I asked Betty Maxwell if she was ever ashamed of him.

'Well, it's more now that I'm ashamed of the picture that's come out. But I was not ashamed of him, no . . . not at the time, although I didn't like his bullying. Towards the end of his life it wasn't shame, it was sadness. I was sad. I was very sorry for him.'

So out of this combination of sorrow and sadness, how did she react to the news of his death?

'I was in Oxford at the time, in our home, Headington Hill Hall. In the beginning when I first heard, I wouldn't believe it. It was a tremendous shock to me. In spite of the fact that we were certainly not as close as we had been earlier on. He was the man of my youth, the man of my life. I loved the man.'

The death of Robert Maxwell might have been a story of personal sorrow and sadness for her but for many people, particularly pensioners in Oxford who had been caught up in the turbulent wake of his life, it was a story of untold distress and disruption. I asked if there was anything that she would like to say to these people.

'I do empathise with them. I feel I knew practically all the staff in Oxford. They were really my friends. They have been enormously decent with me. I can't fault them, the way they have behaved with me afterwards. I'm immensely sorry. All I can hope and pray is that as soon as possible the funds will be replenished and that their anxieties will be lifted. There is nothing else I can do. I wish I had something more positive, but I am myself totally ruined so that physically I can't do for them. But I still love them, and I thank them for all the friendship they gave me for all these thirty-six years that we worked together.'

Betty Maxwell had a powerful grip on the emotional and verbal points of this compass and she could steer a clear course through difficult seas. But did this woman – who lived the life funded by the forlorn futures of pensioners who worked for her husband – did she make a credible case to come across as a caring person?

It's hard to separate the spin from the substance, but she did start to get to me, and I thought maybe – just maybe – the answer might be 'yes'.

Chapter 11

Hounded

Between the foxes and the hounds in the hunting debate.

Children are bad enough, but never broadcast with animals. They must know instinctively that when they're on air they've got the upper hand. You have to behave, they don't. I entertained a pack of fox-hunting hounds during an outside broadcast and they trashed both me and the BBC, and got away scot-free.

Oxfordshire is a rural county, fertile ground for arguments over the banning of fox hunting. So, perhaps unwisely, I decided to host a debate at the largest one-day agricultural show in the country, the Thame Show.

The BBC pushed the boat out and bought in a special trailer for the event, kitted out with a stage, microphones, chairs and bunting with BBC branding all over the place.

It is possible that hounds have an opinion about the BBC?

High noon approached and so did the crowds of people. I didn't see the dogs in the distance. The two hunters and their two opponents took up positions facing each other on stage for the show-down. There was not so much an expectation that a shot would ring out, but rather a general feeling that 'something could happen'.

This was enhanced by an initial incident. An elderly woman supporting the team proposing to ban hunting started to climb onto the stage to give them a notebook. This incensed an elderly fox hunter who tried to stop her. They were both very determined people and didn't want to be seen to be fighting in public. So a discreet boxing match took place. When the woman tried to mount the stage the man, appearing to offer help, actually pulled her off. They were smiling and sweating while doing some pretty fancy footwork, blocking and parrying blows. Eventually one of them tripped and they both fell from sight and weren't seen again before the main bout commenced.

The debate was held on the home turf of the hunters. The Thame Show mainly attracts farmers, fox hunters and the landed gentry. I suspect very few people came to the debate with an open mind. Most people in the audience knew where they stood on this question of banning fox hunting, but I was surprised by the ferocity of the attacks each side made on the other.

One opponent, a woman who farms in the Cotswolds, kicked off the debate. 'The hunt descends on an area without giving us any warning and they can cause chaos even if they don't trespass. We have horses, sheep, cattle and chickens, and if a whole lot of horses arrive in the area with baying dogs and huntsmen with their horns and people overexcited, which they often are when hunting, all shouting and whooping. Your animals are going to get into a pickle and panic. One day my horse was grazing in the paddock and the chickens were all mooching around and suddenly the hunt is around and there is all this electricity going on. My horse goes into a frenzy. They come roaring down the paddock and they crush and kill a chicken and injure another one. The irony of this is that the hunters say they are protecting the countryside and that foxes kill chickens; and yet when the hunt arrives in the area I lose hens.

'Another day the hounds were on cry in the field next to us and ran down the fence line. My horse got in a panic, and ran straight into a fence. The horse died after a few days because she hit the fence with such force. We asked to see the hunt master. His response to this was that our paddock was too small, not that his dogs were running out of control and causing mayhem without telling us that they were going to be here, but that my paddock was too small and I should have had a larger one. It shows you the mind-set that we are up against. It's like the little boy who said, "I didn't break the window, it was the ball." These people live in a different world where you do as you please, you don't have to consider anyone else and you have no conscience and shame to be a hindrance to what you want to do. It's the same as the kids on the council estates who are not worried about authority and what might happen to them. It's the same attitude dressed up in a different uniform, and it's very dangerous, especially when there is a pack of dogs running loose at the same time.'

A master of the hunt in Oxfordshire argued for fox hunting to continue 'because firstly it is a matter of freedom of choice, not only for those who want to go fox hunting, but from the point of view of people who want the fox hunt to cross their land. Secondly I don't see any benefit to the fox population in banning it. And thirdly it is a piece of legislation that is being driven by other factors than animal welfare. It is perceived to be, by a significant number of back-benchers in Parliament, the last bastion of the class war, and it has been publicly stated that they are seeking revenge for how the Thatcher government treated the coal-mining community.'

I wanted to open up the debate and give people listening in the audience direct access to the microphone so I made the mistake of leaping off the stage. The crowd parted and in walked a man dressed in tweeds with a tanned, not to say weather-beaten, face, followed by about twenty-five hounds. He was the huntsman at one of the local hunts, and he controlled the dogs by throwing out bits of white crumbs which they gobbled up. It's possible these were diuretic pills, it's also possible that before he appeared with the dogs he said to them, 'Come on, hounds, let's show the BBC what we think of them.'

The huntsman took the microphone and explained to the crowd how these lovely and lovable tail-wagging dogs would have to be put down if hunting with hounds were banned. 'How could you do that to these innocent animals? Would you like to have that on your conscience?'

He named them, played with them. He gave them orders. They jumped through his hoops. They were delightful, engaging, running circles around everyone, almost mesmerising. Maybe that's why I didn't notice they had jumped on the stage, ripped the bunting and the BBC logo down, chewed it up and left it in tatters, with their calling cards all over the stand. It was pooper-scooper time, big time.

A smart huntsman knows how to make a quick getaway at the right time and within seconds the invaders disappeared. But not before two of them took aim at my legs. My trousers were dripping and so was the microphone lead. I'm sure this was just a bit of high jinks and not an attempt to electrocute me, but it was a bit of hunt sabotage with a difference.

How do you restart a programme after that? Well, you dry yourself off, smile and behave – yes, you always have to behave – as though it were really all rather remarkable fun.

Chapter 12

No Big Issue

Homeless on the mean streets of Oxford.

'Homeless people – forget them. They don't listen to radio. They don't drive the ratings. They're not sexy, and they don't belong on air – unless they've killed someone.' That's the line some radio stations take.

BBC Radio Oxford is not quite so contemptuous and condescending. Every year it has a 'homelessness week'. Each programme on the station looks at the problem, mostly through the eyes of people-in-suits who sit on the boards of charities and write reports, people who talk around a problem they haven't lived through.

I wanted to go for the obvious and invite a homeless person on air to talk about what life is like when you don't have any home or much hope. So I invited Matt, a Glaswegian of no fixed abode living on the streets of Oxford, who sells the one magazine designed to help the homeless, The Big Issue.

Matt and I had talked several times and recently I noticed he was looking a bit the worse for wear. Someone had damaged his eye. It was all black and blue and blurry, as if he might have a permanent problem. He had a story to tell – several. So I invited him to be a co-host on my programme during homelessness week, a sensible, reasonable and logical step, I thought.

Obviously not. My colleagues – 'What? You can't do that! Someone off the street! You just picked a homeless person to be a co-presenter for two or three hours on the BBC. I don't believe it!'

'Why is he homeless? He could have been kicked out of his house because he was a child abuser. He could be on the Sex Offenders Register. He's a possible paedophile.'

'And what about swearing? Can we expect the latest chorus of the 'c' word, the 'f' word and the 'n' word . . . and all with a Glaswegian accent? Is he even articulate, and will he stand up to two or three hours on radio?'

'Will he be coherent? After all he could be on drugs or maybe he'll turn up after a day sitting around getting sozzled on cider.'

They paused for breath so I jumped in. 'No, you've got it wrong. I've heard his story.'

'He could be lying . . .' The team was girding its loins for battle again.

I wasn't exactly sure what particular can of worms I'd opened, but I took a guess. 'Look, I know you have a job to do, but I've checked him out like I check out every one of my co-hosts. They all get equal treatment, whether they be former high court judges or high on drugs, the Foreign Secretary or the Leader of the Opposition or someone who sells The Big Issue on the streets of Oxford.

'I hear where you're coming from and mistakes can happen, even with a co-host of copper-bottomed credentials, like that author who was also a priest, a professor and a theologian. Remember when I was reviewing his new book – *Gays and the Church of England* – and we discussed the humiliating abuse gays had to endure in the past, especially in the Nazi concentration camps. He did take the opportunity to blurt out indignantly on air – "Do you know what the guards called the gays? Bumfuckers!" Now that was an unexpected first and we all probably remember the second when a distinguished Irish publican referred on air to a listener as a "fucking twat". I know all that but it won't happen this time. No nasty surprise in the second layer of this particular chocolate box. Trust me.'

They didn't . . . but we went ahead anyway. I asked Matt on air what it was like to sleep rough in what happened to be a November cold spell with freezing temperatures.

'I used to sleep in a bed at the night shelter in central Oxford, but because of some personal problems I can't go back there; so now I doss down in a shed. It's just four tin walls and a roof on a concrete base. The concrete is the problem.'

'I imagine it's pretty hard,' I said, thinking I was stating the obvious.

'No, that part's OK, but concrete holds the cold. So I collect cardboard, about three big boxes will do. I flatten them out and put my blanket on them, then lie down and fold the blanket and cardboard over me like a sandwich. Just before that I light a small fire. I can sleep for about three hours till the cold kicks in and I wake up with the shivers.

I usually crawl out of my sandwich by six or seven in the morning and try to find some water to wash in. You've got to be as clean as possible if you're going to ask the public to buy The Big Issue. It's pretty lonely. Sometimes in the morning I think I can't get up and face it, but then I can't stay in bed either because I'm freezing. That's one of the big things about being homeless you don't have as many choices . . . and it's lonely.

'I had a partner for a while . . . that was OK, but she hooked up with another bloke who was doing heroin, so our relationship fell apart.'

'You've got quite a shiner; how'd you do that to your right eye?' I said, changing the subject because I guessed we were in a verbal minefield talking about his relationship problems.

'Yes, well I didn't do that. Another thing people don't talk about is the violence that homeless people throw at each other. The myth is that homeless people stick together and support each other. Some do, but there's a lot of violence out on the streets as well and a strong pecking order. Maybe it's because homeless people don't like what's happening to them, and they don't have any power, so they use every opportunity to show their strength. I got pecked.

'Someone with a grudge against me kicked me in the eye. He told me to go away from Oxford and then he punched my lights out. When I was down, he put the boot in. He's a big man and he's got it in for me. I can't go back to the night shelter because he's there and he's threatened me with more violence if I show my face. I can't see very well out of my eye and everything's a haze.'

'Do you think you'll lose it? It's red as hell and looks very angry. Are you angry at what's happened to you?'

'What's the point?' Matt shrugged. 'That's not going to change anything. I've just got to ride this one out. I might lose my sight. We'll just have to wait and see.'

'That's rather philosophical,' I said.

'When you're out on the street, you don't have much else. I mean what am I going to do? Sue him for GBH? Who would take me seriously?'

Matt was a co-host on my programme which meant he could interrupt any interview with a guest and ask his own question. Some co-hosts are intimidated by this power, but not Matt. On the day of his radio debut, one of my guests was Cripa Moya, from Krishna Consciousness in Watford, a group that had obtained a day licence from Oxford City Council to collect money on Cornmarket Street right in the centre of Oxford for their Christmas fundraising campaign. Cripa Moya explained: 'Our members come out from London to sell our books on Indian philosophy to raise a lot of money for our cause. We have a centre in Camden which also serves as a distribution centre for The Big Issue, so the people who sell it get a breakfast and an evening meal. We also have four rickshaws going to deliver hot meals to many London locations.'

Matt – 'So the money collected today in Oxford will go to feed the homeless in London, is that it? I reckon if you are in Oxford collecting the money you should help out local groups like the Gatehouse, the Gap or the Porch, groups that help the homeless in Oxford. Isn't it misleading to collect money in Oxford for homeless people when you know full well that money is going to London?'

The next week Matt stopped me in the street to keep me in the picture. 'Remember you asked me about my eye. Well, I've got the consultant's report and it's a bit "iffy" at the mo, but chances are that I'm not going to lose any sight. I didn't mention on the programme about who did it and why because I didn't want any more problems for me or for you but the bloke who kicked me in the eye was the new boyfriend of my old partner. He was worried that she and I might get back together and he wanted to scare me off. He was probably out of his head on heroin when he went ballistic and attacked me. He's been shooting up for a long time.

'I don't have to worry any more, though. The police found his body two days ago by the staircase in the Westgate car park in central Oxford. He took an overdose. I can't figure if it was a good way to die or not. He was out of it and probably didn't even know he was dying in the most God-forsaken, cold, steel and concrete hole, soaked in urine. Bill, you probably don't know what I'm talking about because you couldn't even dream of dying in a place like that, but for someone who is homeless it's a very real nightmare. I used to be on horse. I know what I'm talking about.'

Matt also wanted to show me his new wardrobe of army waterproof trousers, jumper and coat, his foam sleeping pad and ice-proof, feather-down sleeping bag and a tent he could use in Arctic conditions, which a listener gave him after hearing his story on my programme. 'I can't break my old habits, so I sleep in my clothes and get into my cardboard sandwich, but now instead of a wee blanket I've got this soldier's sleeping bag. I still wake after three hours, but this time it isn't because of the cold, it's because I'm too hot!'

Chapter 13

The Great British Housewife
Desmond Morris on why we still have battery eggs

Animal welfare is a hot topic at Oxford. Debates over how we treat animals have closed down the city centre. One campaign stopped building work for over a year on a new animal experimentation laboratory for Oxford University, and local firms working on it received letters with threats. Protesters forced a local cat breeder out of business after he supplied animals for experiments. Prominent 'pro-experiment' members of the University and their families have received 'home visits', hate mail and packages with detonators in them. All these campaigns were specific and targeted at a few people.

One debate involved nearly everyone and centred on both the chicken and the egg in battery farming. Is this widespread system a cruel abuse of animals, and if so why do we tolerate it?

I invited a group with radically different views on animal rights to discuss the subject on air, including a local battery farmer to set out his stall, a member of the animal liberation movement to challenge him, and Oxford's foremost animal watcher, Desmond Morris.

Peter Humphrey has been a battery farmer for twenty-five years. His farm produces some four million eggs per week – free range, barn eggs and battery. So I asked him what percentage of these are battery eggs and what's the case for battery farming?

'About 90% of our eggs are battery eggs and we produce most of them from the system because quite simply it's the best for the birds. If there were a better way, we would use it. My father started keeping chickens some fifty years ago and they were all on free range then. Gradually he realised that this wasn't very good and kept more and more birds in battery cages.

'We've seen the health of the national flock increase tremendously due to keeping birds in battery cages. The conditions of all the birds are improved. They're provided with all the essentials they require: fresh food, fresh water, a controlled temperature and freedom from predators. They also have greater freedom from diseases. The big advantage is they

*Desmond Morris: 'I don't believe the
housewife...knows the price the chickens are
paying for her eggs.'*

produce very clean, healthy, nutritious eggs, at very good value for the British housewife.'

So from the egg man's view the argument was mainly an economic one about the law of supply and demand. If the housewife demanded something different the farmer would supply eggs the way she wanted it. He was clearly putting her at the centre of the debate, but did she belong there?

I turned 180 degrees to Tim Phillips, editor of a national magazine on animal rights and a vegan, and asked him about the animal liberation movement's direct action tactics, i.e. breaking into battery farms and rescuing animals?

'Well, this is just one of a great number of activities done by individuals. There are all sorts of campaigning in the animal liberation movement, but obviously this is one that generates a great deal of interest. It's very emotive and it grabs headlines, so I'll deal with that; but then I'd like to contest the assertion that the battery system in the best system for the birds.

'The rationale behind the ALM activists who break into factory farms and rescue chickens is that they may be breaking a current law, but they are not breaking what could be termed a higher moral order. In this country some forty million chickens are held in battery cages. They can't stretch their wings out. They're standing on a wire mesh sloping floor. They can't do anything that's natural to them – dust-bathing, stretching their wings, running, even getting sunlight. They have to lay their eggs in front of all their colleagues rather than go to a nest box and do it in private. And it's understandable that people are outraged by that and wish to alleviate the suffering of individual birds.

'In a way it is tokenism, because you are talking about people rescuing say twenty birds in a unit that holds perhaps, 20,000 birds . . .'

Peter Humphrey, the battery farmer, broke in here with an icy fury. 'There can be no justification at all for illegal acts in this country. British farmers take great care – look after their animals with great care.'

Tim Phillips tried to continue. 'Can I finish please?'

But the battery farmer was in no mood to back down. 'We operate within the law under codes that are laid down and carefully thought out by Her Majesty's Government. There can be no justification for law breaking within the UK.'

Tim Phillips was philosophical. 'It's undeniable that the law will eventually be changed on this. I think if someone's great-great-grandfather had rescued a cockerel that was to be forced to cock-fight the next day, it would be now looked on very warmly and nostalgically.'

I invited Desmond Morris to assess the debate and I knew he wouldn't pull any punches.

'As a student of animal behaviour, I personally find it an ugly system, and I use that word advisedly. It's an aesthetic statement of mine . . . I'm not talking about economics. I'm talking about aesthetics. I find the restraint of an animal – and we're talking here of five birds to a cage, eighteen inches by twenty inches, that gives each bird a space approximately the size of an A4 sheet of typing paper to live on throughout its entire life – now I find that ugly; and I am personally prepared to pay the few pence extra to have a free range egg. That's my personal choice.

'My main objection as a zoologist is the clandestine way in which the system is run; and by clandestine what I mean is that I don't believe the housewife that Peter has mentioned knows the price the chickens are paying for her eggs. I think that if she were aware of the system she might be prepared to pay a few pence extra. What I require as a zoologist who buys eggs to eat, is a simple stamp put on the eggs which says B for Battery and F for Free Range. I want that freedom of choice, and I don't want to be deceived by labels saying 'fresh farm eggs' with pictures of a beautiful countryside scene, which I consider actually to be breaking the law with regard to advertising.'

Once again she appears almost as a ghost haunting the debate – the great British housewife, so I asked Desmond his view on whether the housewife up the Cowley Road in Oxford would actually care if she knew how chickens were treated.

'I would like to try and make her care, and I would like to suggest to her that those few extra pennies could mean a reduction in the exploitation of the chicken's behaviour.

'It's a matter of education. We must let people know what these systems are and then let them decide what they want to pay for. You have to pay a few pennies extra, but I, as a student of zoology, am prepared to do that.

The egg man was adamant. 'No, that is wrong. The free range system is a much more costly way of producing eggs. There's no doubt about that. One man can look after about 20,000 birds in cages. It needs one man to look after about 2,500 birds in traditional free range.'

Desmond Morris confessed that he found it hard to look after just a few pets. 'Any man who is expected to look after 20,000 animals means those 20,000 animals can't be very well looked after by the nature of human behaviour.'

The battery farmer challenged Desmond. 'You say it's bad for the birds. What is your criterion for saying the battery system is bad for the birds?'

Desmond Morris: 'My criteria are based on studies of domestic fowl when I was a zoologist here at Oxford many years ago, and I looked at their behaviour. I am aware of the fact that you mentioned food, water, temperature and absence of predators as the good news for these birds. But the bad news is a much longer list. The bad news is a deprivation of a whole range of behaviour patterns. Having been a curator at a zoo, I have studied the response of animals to a restricted environment. And I've studied the way in which, when you simplify an environment for an animal, it produces all kinds of aberrant behaviour patterns and produces a whole range of behaviours that we would call abnormal.

'I've seen birds in battery cages after they had been there for a long time. When the cage doors were opened, the birds hung back and scrambled into a far corner. They were confused and disoriented. There was an eerie feeling like those pictures of Auschwitz and Belsen after the Allied troops came and liberated the camps. At first people didn't want to come out.'

Tim Phillips from the animal liberation movement – 'It seems to me that we can't say birds in these tiny cages don't suffer – they do. And perhaps we've reached the end of that line of argument. Now I'd say they definitely do suffer and the main debate is can we justify that, which is the main defence we've heard today, simply for saving a few pence on eggs. Are we prepared to have systems which are cruel simply because they are economically viable?'

I knew at the heart of this subject there was a great deal of passion as well as prejudice. I wanted to find out, with regard to the prejudice, if any of the contributors had changed their views.

Peter Humphrey, the battery farmer: 'Yes, of course, we're always very receptive and know the concern of the housewife in particular about buying her food. We will continue to research better ways to keep our hens. We've been doing research for the last ten years and spending a lot of money on research. Secondly, I think I must take Desmond Morris shopping and show him all the clearly labelled free range eggs, barn eggs and fresh eggs that are available in the shops.'

When he mentioned the great British housewife again I was beginning to wonder if this creature was real or mythical. Right on cue Susan Marshall, a granny and secretary of the Oxfordshire Animal Welfare Society, contacted the programme and put her head above the parapet. 'I can promise the egg man that the up-and-coming generation wants to have free range and they want no truck with battery systems. A hen needs a comfortable nesting box, an area where she can scratch and walk about and have a dust bath and flap her wings. She was clearly not created for the battery system, and it is surely a measure of our meanness that we deny her even these modest needs.'

Tim Phillips from the animal liberation movement: 'Obviously I know that this suffering is completely unnecessary. We can wrap it up and say it is necessary because people want to do it. But discussions like this one always confirm to me just how far there is to go before we start educating people gradually that they don't need these products. When you go to supermarkets, get the free range, if you really have to have eggs.'

And the final word went to Desmond Morris. 'Peter said he would take me shopping and show me the label with free range eggs. What I would love him to do is to show me the ones labelled "battery" because, you see, the trouble is that they're ashamed of calling them battery eggs and they love calling them free range eggs. The free range eggs are all beautifully labelled because that's good news, but the battery ones, they just say "fresh farm eggs".'

And why do we tolerate that? According to almost every contributor it all boils down to the mighty economic power of the great British housewife who wants cheap food. Is this sensitive, animal-loving creature the real reason we still have battery chickens and eggs, or is she too just a foil in this fowl game?

Chapter 14

Uncovering the Plot
Investigating the trail of a paedophile.

A BBC local radio presenter has a passport to travel between worlds that exist side by side – the underworld of the criminals and the realm of those above-board. They rarely connect but if you find a way to cross over the results can shock. People who commit crimes sometimes have a sense of honour. They often judge each other. They punish each other. They stand up for what they see as right and wrong and they have an ethical code. I met a man who served time for attempted rape and crossed over to become an example to the rest of us, but first he took me into his world.

Joe served five and a half years in Bullingdon Prison near Oxford and had been listening to my radio programmes; some of them focused on his case. When he got out he rang to introduce himself and asked to meet up 'because you've got some of your facts wrong and maybe I can help'. I was intrigued – either he was unhinged and wanted to punch my eyes out or he was on the level and had something to say.

We met and hit it off. Joe was a big, hard man, 6'4" tall, well built, 16 stone, and he knew how to throw a punch, which he didn't do. Just coming out of prison, he was at a loose end, and I happened to be starting a charity swim from Oxford to London and needed someone to count my laps. I enlisted Joe and we spent the next three months getting to know each other.

He talked about his trial and the charge of attempted rape, which he's never admitted, and his time in prison when he went through the Sexual Offenders Treatment Programme – a 'don't blink' look at what sexual offenders do, how it affects the victims and how they can reduce the risks of re-offending. After the course he was trained by the Samaritans as a 'prison listener' and visited inmates on different landings who were heading towards suicide. He also formed a 'landing committee' to deal with bullying and abuse on the Rule 43 Landing for vulnerable prisoners – schizophrenics, paedophiles and psychopaths.

One of the inmates Joe had helped on the Rule 43 Landing recently came out of prison and settled in Oxford because he wanted Joe to protect him if he got into trouble outside. Mark was a paedophile and latched onto Joe as a friend. Joe agreed to have a few drinks with Mark on the proviso that Mark started a new life and kept away from children. They stayed in contact and things were going well until one day Mark asked Joe to persuade me to use my programme on BBC Radio Oxford to uncover a plot against him. He wanted to lodge a complaint against the Thames Valley Police for kicking down the door to his flat and confiscating some of his professional work – photographs.

I met Mark, and with Joe's help I gained access to all his records. This is the plot we uncovered.

On 22 January 1999, Mark walked out of Bullingdon prison after serving three and a half years for sex offences, fraud and perverting the course of justice. He had £52 in his pocket and a bed for the night at an Oxford probation hostel. He needed a better address to establish himself and obtain credit, to get back into business, to get near children . . . and he succeeded in full public view. This is not a tale of a sex offender changing his name, going underground and preying on children. This is how one man openly defied, manipulated or slipped through all the safety nets of all the authorities who had a responsibility to stop him.

Mark soon found a flat in Oxford's up-market town-house development of Green Ridges in Headington for £560 per month, located twenty-five yards away from the grounds of two schools, the Barton Village First School and the Omerod Special School with 208 pupils between them aged from three to nine years. He would pass both schools to enter or leave Green Ridges.

Who helped Mark get the flat? Two respected charities. The English Churches Housing Group stepped in to support his application for the new address. This helped him get housing benefit of £470 per month from the Oxford City Council. Then the Oxford Lord Mayor's Deposit Scheme, designed to help vulnerable people get a place to live, agreed to guarantee Mark's monthly net rental payments of £90 and put up a Lord Mayor's Bond of £560 for his initial deposit, which enabled Mark to move in. Charity workers can be so eager to help their clients get one rung up the ladder they don't see where the ladder leads.

The Family Protection Unit of the Thames Valley Police, probation officers and social service staff would all be involved in the decision to re-house a man, on the Sex Offenders Register for taking indecent photographs of children, in an area that was a Mecca for families with children.

The address was the key to Mark's plan. Now he needed clients: children, preferably from single-parent families, children with mothers who needed money. He would persuade parents to hand over their children by promising to turn them into models and movie stars. Mark started up a child model agency even while he was still on licence from prison and being monitored by a parole officer.

All this time Mark was under supervision by the police and had been assessed by a team of psychologists and psychiatrists as 'posing a serious threat to others, particularly those who are vulnerable by age or by the level of threat Mark perceives them as posing to himself', such as mothers who reported Mark to the police.

Adverts appeared around the country – 'Do you have a child or children who you think could be a model? If you think so, we are currently looking for children aged between six months and eighteen years for a newly formed professional modelling agency'.

The Yellow Pages for Central London and Oxford accepted the adverts. He ran up a bill for £20,738.69 on the 'Talking Pages' for a slice of the country covering Aylesbury to Banbury, Oxford and Reading, Wokingham to High Wycombe and the West End and City of London. The ads even appeared in national children's charity promotions like K.I.N.D. (Kids in Need and Distress) who charged him £445.00 plus VAT. Do advertising departments carry out elementary checks on people who are 'looking for children'? Did they know he was a Schedule One sex offender who had just come out of prison and was entered on the Sex Offenders Register?

With this publicity in place Mark had primed the pump, but how could he start it without any money? Mark was collecting £52.20 each week from the government's Job Seekers Allowance scheme plus housing benefit and help with his council tax. From this slender economic base he ordered two digital video cameras for £47,000, plus several cameras with an array of lenses, laboratory equipment, office supplies and furniture, a car, various telephone systems, a special fibre optics cable to his flat, a laptop and other state-of-the-art computers.

He also set up a website that would serve two purposes: to advertise his agency and to sell the images of children he would collect. The company Mark employed for this offered him an 'active' website where the information on his pages would constantly be updated. The total cost was £2,571.50 with £381.50 VAT.

Mark signed all the contracts, received the equipment and the invoices; but very little money, if any, changed hands. Just like with the advertising, Mark got the ads placed in the media and he got the invoices, but the publicity departments did not necessarily get paid. The invoices are valuable because they provide the link to the next organisation he used to fund his operation: the tax system.

Banks wouldn't give him credit, so Mark turned to a source that had proved helpful to various prison acquaintances in the past – the VAT office. He was starting a business, and in the first, second and possibly third VAT quarters he might have no income and could therefore reclaim all the VAT on his purchases.

On all his invoices, which he could not pay because he had no resources, he added a stamp confirming the bill was 'paid in full'. Supported by this crude documentation, he claimed his total expenditure was about £160,000 and therefore submitted VAT returns claiming two refunds, one for £8,264.73 and another of around £20,000. The VAT office simply paid up. If they had bothered to check any details, tax officials would have found that the man claiming to have spent £160,000 was still drawing the Job Seekers Allowance. Further, they would have discovered that he had come out of prison months earlier for fraud convictions.

But no signals flashed, and Mark sailed through the system, perhaps close to the wind, but certainly closer to children. He now had everything he needed – an established base, national publicity, equipment and public funding of £28,000 to develop his child model agency. Mark did not even need a licence. The Department of Trade and Industry used to run a licensing system for those who wanted to set up child model agencies, but that was scrapped in 1995.

His model business flourished. The website had thousands of hits and the phones rang constantly. Mark ran up and down the country photographing children from Southampton to Leeds.

The deal was simple. Mark offered to take photographs of children and market them as models, in return for a fee of £176 for the pictures, registration fee and enrolment fee in his agency. He photographed thousands of children, kept the copyright to the pictures and collected the fees, yet there is no evidence he got even one child employment as a model.

Mark abused not only the trust of the parents. Ryan and Shane are brothers aged eight and seven. Mark visited them at home to photograph them. Since one shot was to feature Ryan as 'Rambo', Mark sent their mother out of the room for black boot polish.

This is her account: 'On my return I found Ryan sat on Mark's knee in a pair of jeans with no T-shirt. I gave Mark the polish and he applied the make-up to Ryan's face, body, arms and back. I was in and out of the room leaving Mark with Ryan and Shane on their own. Towards the end of the session Mark appeared to be a nervous wreck: he was shaking all over and could not even hold his coffee cup. Later I mentioned Mark's name to Shane and he said: "I don't like him . . . he smacks Ryan on the bum".'

The Rambo picture also features in the experience of Adam, another seven-year-old. Adam's mother, a single parent, put her son's name down for a modelling agency to help 'make ends meet' and invited Mark into her home to take 'numerous photographs of Adam wearing different costumes. One of which was a pair of my knickers, which Adam wore as a g-string, that Mark had cut up to give this impression'. Mark went on to indecently assault Adam.

Matthew, seven, claims Mark took him and his two brothers home to the flat at Green Ridges in Oxford where he led Matthew into the bathroom, locked the door, exposed himself and proceeded to assault the boy. On the strength of Matthew's evidence, a case was brought against Mark in court.

While this case was proceeding, Mark made several court appearances.

Each time the magistrates granted him bail on conditions that allowed him to continue with his child model agency and photography.

In spite of his previous conviction for taking indecent photographs of children, the police asked for no restrictions on Mark's activities, even though they had received complaints about his photography and had recently kicked in a door to raid his Oxford flat at Green Ridges taking away hundreds of photographs and negatives. The police did not ask Mark to surrender his passport. No warning lights flashed for the police, the courts and the Crown Prosecution Service to stop Mark. He continued his child model agency for a further three months, amassed more enrolment fees, photographs and VAT refunds.

As the final court date loomed, Mark calmly boarded a plane in Luton for Tenerife because he said he had lost faith in the British system of justice. He didn't think he would receive a fair trial, even though so far he had received every break and benefit the system had to offer.

In Tenerife, Mark found employment with a 'glamour' modelling agency and stayed with English criminals on the run. They took his money, ran off with his car and rifled through his belongings where they found Mark's photographs of children, and they became incensed. Two men took him to the beach and gave him a punishment beating that put him in hospital for several days. They also told him to leave the island or he would die.

On his release from hospital, Mark was kicked out of his flat and lost his job with the 'glamour' photography studio. All his cameras and computers were gone.

In the space of three months he was reduced to begging for food and sleeping rough on the beach in cardboard boxes during December. In desperation Mark caught a flight back to Luton. Informants gave police details of Mark's flight and an officer from the Thames Valley Police Family Protection Unit arrested him at the airport. This time magistrates remanded him to prison.

The trial took place in Oxford Crown Court five months later than it should have. Mark argued that Matthew and his brothers were simply not at his flat. He had a statement from his mother saying she stayed with her son at the flat and saw no children on the date the alleged attack took place. However, his mother, a devout Catholic, refused to attend court to give evidence.

Matthew, the key witness, was eight years old by now and under questioning by Mark's barristers gave contradictory replies. The judge informed the jury she would not be seeking a guilty verdict and the trial collapsed.

So Mark was back in business again, this time photographing children for a national chain called Olan Mills in Tilehurst near Reading. Parents would register at the studio reception and receive a docket with their address, telephone numbers and name and age of their children, which they gave to Mark. He used this information to build up a database of potential private customers for himself. Mark was fired after several months and several hundred dockets had passed through his hands.

He was on the street again looking for further opportunities to use his camera. He picked up some work photographing a children's football team in East Barnet, north London, and put in bids to become the school photographer at several north London primary schools. But he had several channels to children and one eye on the 'lonely hearts columns'.

Debbie from Wales said she was looking for a caring man who would be a good role model for her seven-year-old son Tom. Mark started visiting Debbie on the weekends, treating the family to meals. He was the perfect gentleman and far from being put off by the fact that she had a child, he took special interest in Debbie's son Tom. Mark started to stay overnight and slept in the bottom part of Tom's bunk-bed.

Joe was in telephone contact with Mark at this time and one weekend Mark rang to say – 'I don't know what's gong on. Tom says he wants to kill himself. I must be involved with a very mixed-up family'. Alarm bells rang for Joe and he asked where Mark was, said goodbye and rang the Thames Valley Police to warn them that Mark would be grooming and molesting another seven-year-old boy.

The police responded quickly this time which frightened Mark off. He raced back to his home in the Thames Valley only to find all his belongings in black bin bags on the kerb in front of his house. His father had disowned him after reading an article I wrote about Mark's activities published in *The Sunday Times* that same day. Mark's house of cards had collapsed.

Joe rang the VAT office and alerted them to a possible fraud. They confirmed that the payment to Mark had been approved and was being processed for payment. On the basis of Joe's information, they agreed to look again at Mark's claim.

Within days and before he got any money, lit a match or fired a bullet, Mark was arrested on charges of indecent assault against a seven-year-old child and VAT fraud and put on remand in Gloucester Prison.

During the time he was on the run, Mark rang my Radio Oxford programme to accuse me on air of trying to destroy him. He then rang Joe with a modest proposal. The two of them could escape to Ireland. Mark had a £623,000 payment coming from the VAT office after submitting a claim for expenses totalling £3,560,000, and he would give Joe £100,000 if Joe would set fire to Debbie's house and 'take out that woman and her son' and then shoot me.

Chapter 15

The Threat Thickens
How do you live with a death threat?

Broadcasters of regularly scheduled programmes, especially broadcasters with sharks in their roofs, are sitting ducks if someone wants to bump them off. Their work patterns are well known and so are their home addresses. But I had an ace up my sleeve in the curious incident of that death threat by Mark because Joe, my intended assassin, was also my friend. When Mark swung into murderous mode with the ease of Tarzan reaching out for another grapevine, Joe was on hand to protect me.

I lost my ace when Mark was put on remand at Gloucester Prison for child abuse and VAT fraud. He was looking at a long sentence if convicted and he met two other people on remand accused of crimes of pretty heavy violence. They had already received twelve-year sentences and would be sent down for life if found guilty this time.

They hatched a plan to help each other by switching over hit lists. Mark would arrange for his man to take out their witnesses and they would reciprocate by instructing their friends to finish off Mark's problem people. This would remove the motive from the murders.

Mark's problem people included Tom, the seven-year-old boy he was accused of sexually assaulting, Debbie, the mother who reported it, and me, the man who knew too much.

Mark wanted Debbie and Tom petrol-bombed. He knew they slept upstairs and wanted the killers to soak the downstairs hall of their house with petrol, through the letterbox, and then throw petrol bombs through two windows, one into the ground-floor lounge and another into the hall with the only staircase leading upstairs. There would be little chance of Tom or Debbie escaping. To Mark that was the end of it – no witnesses, no trial.

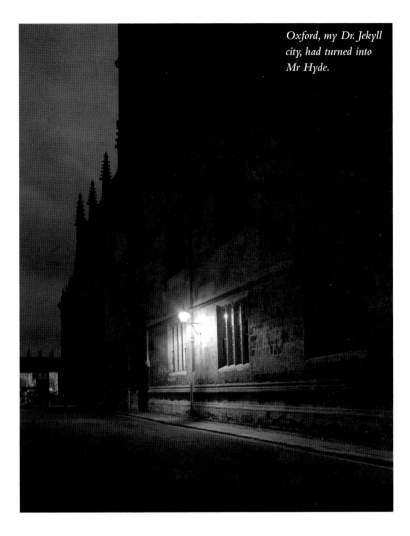

Oxford, my Dr. Jekyll city, had turned into Mr Hyde.

Joe summarised the plot: 'Mark, you are burning them to death'. The answer: 'I couldn't care less as long as I get out of this prison.'

Mark also had a problem with me because I exposed his activities in that Sunday Times article. Joe told me, 'He had always wanted to even it up with you and have you shot. The plan before he was arrested and sent on remand to Gloucester Prison was that he and I would leave the country after your murder. He was deadly serious. He wanted to catch you coming out of the BBC after your programme and put a bullet in your brain.

'When he went into one of these fantasies I would inform the police that he was off his head again, but you were safe. When he played this death game with killers in the nick, the situation would be dangerous for you.'

Mark gave out the addresses of Debbie, Tom and me to the hit men of his co-conspirators together with diagrams of our houses and then asked Joe to carry out his part of the pact and kill the other peoples' witnesses. At first Joe thought the murder plots were little more than 'landing talk' with no substance, but when Mark gave him the telephone numbers of a conspirator's girlfriend who would point out the people he was to do in, Joe went to the police.

They immediately moved Tom and Debbie to a safe house and wanted to wire up Joe with tape-recording equipment, but he declined the invitation on the basis that this would expose his role and make him a future target for Mark. The police urged Joe to visit Mark in prison, find out where the plot was heading and bring out evidence for a court case on conspiracy to pervert the course of justice.

This conspiracy wasn't heading anywhere because Joe was the lynchpin. But Mark still had the upper hand. The co-conspirators were more desperate than Mark. They needed someone to finish off their witnesses immediately. So he could push their buttons because time was on his side not theirs. Mark asked his 'friends' to prove to him they were serious, that they could get things done. So the log jam on the conspiracy broke . . . at my house.

One afternoon, two unusual visitors came by to survey the site. My neighbours directly opposite were so used to seeing thousands of people viewing the shark in my roof that they didn't even notice the stream of visitors anymore.

This day though these men caught my neighbour's eye. 'Two big bruisers stood around outside your home for quite awhile and went down the side drive to the back. They weren't here to see the shark; they didn't smile or look at the roof, only the door and windows. I went across and asked what they were doing. Neither of them said anything. Very rude. They just glared at me. The look that came out of the bald one was evil. They walked over to their car, a vintage Jag XJ6, and drove away immediately, all the time looking at me and glaring.'

Some days later a gang smashed one of the rear windows of my house (with a modus operandi that the police had not seen before in the Oxford area) and searched my property.

Joe had a pretty clear idea of what was going on: 'You had some visitors who were doing two things – searching for you and searching for the twelve hours of video tape you had after filming Mark talking about his photography and fantasies in England and on the run in Tenerife. They were going to do you. They wanted to kill you. I don't know what your movements were that night, but you could well have had a reception committee waiting for you.'

The gang was never caught, but for months the police put sensors in my house to detect movement and this was linked to an incident room at their local headquarters.

The conspiracy went pear-shaped. All the 'partners' pointed fingers at each other. The trials went ahead with all the witnesses; nobody was killed. Mark pleaded guilty to sexual abuse because his barrister said there was no real defence if the seven-year-old boy stuck to his story. Mark also pleaded guilty to VAT fraud. The judge gave him an eight-year sentence on each charge to run concurrently. Mark collapsed in court and was carried out on a stretcher to the prison hospital.

My life went slightly pear-shaped too. How do you live with a death threat? It affects the people you love, the person you want to be, and the people who could be at your graveside. Every aspect of your life is under scrutiny.

Why was I in this situation? Because I wanted to stop other people – children – from becoming victims of a paedophile. I exposed his activities and helped put him behind bars, and by doing that I put myself in the firing line and became a victim myself.

What did I think of that bargain? Did it make sense? Was it fair? Everyday I woke up and said, 'No'. I screamed, 'No'. I was angry.

But who was to blame for the fact that I was in the frame? How could I write a detailed exposé of a paedophile in a major newspaper and think it would have no consequences? It was an unwise thing to have done from many points of view.

And why didn't I read the signals along the way? I knew Mark could be a viper and attack. The risk assessment I quoted earlier said Mark 'could pose a significant risk to others, particularly those who are vulnerable by age or by the level of threat Mark perceives them as posing to himself", such as the mothers who report him to the police. What about journalists who did the same thing? Why didn't I see the threat coming? It couldn't have been a surprise, I had all the clues. Was it a case of arrogance – no one would dare attack me – or stupidity – I didn't know what would happen but, of course, it couldn't possibly be a death threat?

When you know someone wants to kill you, has put out a contract on your life, you're not dealing with paranoia, you're dealing with fact; and it focuses the mind. You pare things down to the core, to what really matters; and as with so much of this story it comes down to children. But now it was my own eleven-year-old child. It was the bloom on his cheek in the morning when I woke and he was still asleep. It was that direct connection between openness and innocence that catches you for a moment or more when you linger at the bottom of the bed in quiet communication. It's that very thread I wanted to protect in other children that I might be destroying in my own child.

If someone shot me what would that do to him? It's all very nice to ask, 'How do I live with a death threat?', but how does he live with my death – 'I'm sorry but you don't have a father anymore; he was killed because he was protecting other children'? A father's first responsibility is to protect his own child. So how do you weigh that balance? 'Why doesn't my son have a father' against 'why don't potential victims have their innocence'? And of course it could have all been a double negative: I could have been shot and Mark could have gone on to abuse hundreds of children. That was his plan. Then what would the tally card have looked like?

Other, smaller, concerns emerged – cars, shadows and crowds, for starters. One morning at seven when I came out of the front door, I noticed a car opposite the drive, just standing there with the engine running. It was cold. I could clearly see the exhaust. Inside was a thin solitary man looking in my direction. He raised his arm. I had closed and locked the door behind me so I couldn't escape quickly that way. There was no place to go but straight ahead. I had one of those 'this-is-it' moments and took cover behind a small brick wall.

The car door opened and a voice called out, 'I'm glad I wasn't too late to catch you.' It was the voice of my host from a dinner party the night before. I'd left my car at his house and taken a taxi home. He had suggested he would fetch me in the morning. I thought it was only a gesture of generosity. But no, here he was smiling on my doorstep at the crack of dawn, accidentally exposing a crack in my mental make-up. I thanked him profusely. 'You really shouldn't have done it.'

The friendly, familiar face of the city I knew and loved so well also altered. Oxford's High Street is one of the most beautiful in the world, but now, especially at night, it took on a different character. The walkways leading to the Radcliffe Camera, Logic Lane, the steps leading to The Queen's College, the entrance to the Examination Schools, the rose bushes at the Botanic Garden and the bastions and benches on Magdalen Bridge merited a second look, not aimed at appreciating their beauty but their danger. My Dr Jekyll city had turned into Mr Hyde.

Crowds and queues were now more than inconvenient. Crowds could conceal someone with a gun and a queue meant I was a standing target. Even restaurants were slightly unsettling. I sat in the corner chair facing the door and other diners, so I could react quickly.

I wasn't the only person strolling around in no man's land. Joe was a fellow traveller: 'Mark was on a strange landing with a lot of weird people and a fair share of psychos coming through and some of them being released. The more he talked to these people the more chance they might say something like – "Mark, you were hanging around with Joe and everything you did went haywire. He's the cause of your downfall". Of course, anyone could see that except Mark because he was too involved with me. I was the only person to talk to him. But I was worried that finally he would finger me.

'I said to the police that this guy is dangerous when he approaches people with these wild plans and people believe him. When he susses what I've done to him, he will come after me or ask people to kill me.

'The police talked about me going into a safe house, and they wanted to put me into witness protection so I changed my name and lost connection with my kids. The police offered me that but I declined. For a while I was cautious and I thought if it's going to come around it will come around soon enough. I kept my head down and watched my back.'

That was the state of alert when Mark successfully appealed against his eight-year sentence at the Old Bailey and got it reduced to four years. This meant that with remission for good behaviour he would be out on the streets again in two months. Officially he was getting points for good behaviour because the police couldn't show their hand and reveal the death plots without implicating Joe.

Mark was euphoric . . . for a very short time. Unexpectedly he came down with a bad case of blood poisoning and ended up in the prison hospital with only three pints of blood in his system, or so Joe was told. The next week Joe received a telephone call from Mark's mother. She was distraught.

Mark had died in hospital. She asked Joe if he would mind not coming along to the funeral because the family wanted a quiet, private affair.

It was all somewhat bizarre and mysterious. Try finding out how someone in prison died – it's treated as a state secret. We never did find out what really happened. There were a lot of unanswered questions.

So how did I react to the news of Mark's death? There are a few layers to peel off here. We're supposed to be sad at the death of someone – anyone. We all share a common thread of humanity and we owe those who have died respect and dignity and a farewell to the loss of future promise.

I wasn't sad, and this was a new reaction to death on my part. I didn't grieve, in fact I felt relieved. I can accept that the death of a person who had put out a contract on my life might be a cause to pause and give thanks. But there is a big gulf between thanksgiving and joy. I was delighted at Mark's death. To me it meant that he would not pose a threat to any more seven-year-olds or to Debbie, Tom and me.

How do I feel about dancing on someone's grave? I've never done that before and I never thought I would. I was uncomfortable; I had a heavy heart. But to me Mark's death was a win–win situation.

Could he, would he, have changed? How do you pick the power of redemption out of those bones? Did I betray anything in myself through my joy at someone else's death? What did I lose when Mark lost his life?

Chapter 16

A Bit of a Miracle
Colin Dexter and Inspector Morse

Colin Dexter and I were doing a television interview about the filming of a new series – Lewis, a follow-on from his stories about Inspector Morse. We were in the Fellows' Garden of Exeter College, distinguished mainly by the view from the top of a mound. It provided an operatic backdrop that revealed the dome of one of Oxford's most magnificent buildings, the Radcliffe Camera. The production team went to a great deal of effort to make the city of Oxford a main character in the Morse films, so naturally the TV people wanted this kind of setting for Colin's interview.

The crew ambled up the steps of the mound to set up a shot. Colin and I began the climb together. He leaned over and asked if he could possibly hold my arm and mentioned something about heights and hearing. It was a cold spring morning and the steps were glistening with a little white frost. I could see the crocuses were struggling and even the daffodils looked a little ill. In these conditions anyone might slip and fall.

While we were hobbling up this Wagnerian ascent with me on his 'good' side – the right – our conversation turned to Inspector Morse. I mentioned the last episode, *The Remorseful Day*, and suggested that the title was pretty near perfect.

'I couldn't resist it, I'm afraid. That's such a lovely poem by Housman.' Then on this grey spring morning in Oxford, mounting a slippery slope turtle-like, he turned towards me with those piercing dark eyes and that far-away half-smile and gave me a gift. With frosted breath, a pause now and then for balance and a tightening grip, his voice and the words made the sky change hue. Suddenly in those few short steps it wasn't misty, damp and murky, but sharp, crisp and fiery.

How clear, how lovely bright,
How beautiful to sight
Those beams of morning play;
How Heaven laughs out with glee
Where, like a bird set free,
Up from the eastern sea
Soars the delightful day.

Today I shall be strong,
No more shall yield to wrong,
Shall squander life no more;
Days lost, I know not how,
I shall retrieve them now;
Now I shall keep the vow
I never kept before.

Ensanguining the skies
How heavily it dies
Into the west away;
Past touch and sight and sound
Not further to be found,
How hopeless under ground
Falls the remorseful day.

When he finished we were both quiet for a moment and then he grinned. 'I love that – "ensanguining the skies". Where does that come from? It's magical. And the hope, the certainty that today is the day, it all changes now: "squander life no more, keep the vow I never kept before". The brightness of it and then gradually, but surely the darkness, the undoing of the day, the despair of another day lost . . . until again those beams of morning play.'

By the time we reached the top of that mound we knew we had been on a journey; and we came back to earth with a jolt. He took his hand off my arm but he wasn't ready to let go of The Remorseful Day, perhaps because we were in the grounds of the very college where Morse had his fatal heart attack. It was here that Colin Dexter killed off the character he'd lived with for thirty odd years – almost another

Colin Dexter and I at the Randolph Hotel in central Oxford, a favourite haunt of Inspector Morse.

self to him. To kill that other self must have been an event. But it was more than that; he was also calling time on a phenomenally valuable and successful series, a landmark of British TV.

Colin reminded me that the poem played a small part in the last episode. 'Morse recited it fairly slowly, word perfect in one take. John Thaw did it beautifully, as always. When I last rang him thirteen days before he died, he said he wasn't sure he was the greatest actor in the world, but he knew there was one thing he could do better than the vast majority of his colleagues on TV, radio, film and stage – learn his lines more accurately. He told me: "I'm sitting here now learning my lines for the next episode of Kavanagh QC. I'm feeling better and the consultants are delighted."

'John and Kevin [Whateley] were sitting outside the Victoria Arms in Old Marston, each with a pint of beer, overlooking the River Cherwell and the water-meadows to the west. John didn't even like beer, by the way. It was six or seven, latish summer. As John was reciting, the great orange ball of the sun was, so very gradually, sinking below the western horizon.

'Between Kevin and John in the sunset and this wonderful marriage of voice and vision there was a depth that made the poem different. People standing around listening were very moved. There was a profound sense that something was happening here. Certainly the producer, Chris Burt, thought it was a bit of a miracle.

'The poem is a commentary by Housman on human nature. Some would say about him, why don't you cheer us up instead of playing fiddle to the dying cow? But this poem is not a saddened reflection of life. It's a charming poem with a wry humour so unusual in AEH. The theme of the poem is "remorse", yes, but remorse for unfulfilled intentions, the "I'll do it tomorrow" philosophy. It is beautifully set, these three verses, in terms of the opening and closing of any day: the beams of early morn to the orange band of eve. And I suppose it was a miraculous moment when we had that coincidence of the setting of the sun and the awakening of the words. It just happened that one afternoon at exactly the right time.'

Chapter 17

A Diabolic City
Visiting Oxford in a wheelchair.

'Moaning Minnies . . . the airwaves are clogged with them, these creepy crawlies who can't stand up for themselves, grab the telephone, get instant access to the airwaves and let it all hang out, their anger, impotence and frustration at something trivial that most of us don't give a damn about. Cut them off. Don't give them airspace and time. We've heard it all before. It's boring.' I get this advice from some listeners.

The airwaves create a pretty democratic space where people with special needs can highlight problems that are often ignored. But 'creepy crawlies who can't stand up for themselves'? Mary rang to say, '"Walking will be difficult," my doctor told me. It would be like a prison . . . I couldn't post a letter or buy milk when I ran short. I couldn't exercise my dog.' She put her passion about the problem into a poem called Buggy Riders. Here's a flavour:

> *So I got myself a buggy*
> *Took note of driving codes*
> *Found out all the problems*
> *Of our neglected roads.*
> *Shaken by sunken manholes*

I knew the world of the wheelchair user was a foreign land, but one I wanted to explore. When I almost bumped into a scooter in Oxford city centre, the driver, Reg, recognised me and said, 'Bill, you should put your backside into one of these things and find out what it's like to see the world from three feet lower, on wheels', so I jumped to it.

Robin Brooks is head of the Oxford Shopmobility Scheme that offers eighteen scooters and six powered wheelchairs free to people who have difficulty walking and want to get around Oxford. He rang my radio programme with a public invitation to 'see Oxford from a

Oxford's transport supremo David Robertson with me – the beginning of a journey to discover a 'world from three feet lower, on wheels.'

different view'. I persuaded the political boss in charge of travel and transport on the County Council, David Robertson, to join me; and we both went on a trip through the looking glass.

David and I emerged in our scooters from the basement of the Westgate Car Park in Central Oxford like two newly hatched goslings suddenly thrust into a strange world and definitely out of our comfort zone. The first obstacle was a car ramp with a steep gradient. Even though the engines were powerful, we found it difficult to mount the hill and had to weave the scooters back and forth to get up the slope. Two men meandering up the middle of an exit ramp would be an easy target. If any car had come quickly, our goose would have been pan fried with a knob of butter!

When we reached level ground in the centre of Oxford the top man responsible for organising travel and transport was candid: 'People in the streets were courteous and kept out of the way, but maybe they were frightened that I would run them down. I think we chose the wrong day to negotiate the pavements of Oxford. The city's refuse was put out for collection, so bins and black bags were strewn all over the footpaths, well, not strewn, more strategically placed to loom bigger than life for someone in a scooter. We hit a forest of cardboard boxes that refused to stay in place or out of the way. And the advertisements, those 'A' boards, were abysmal.'

I agreed. If we were walking, we could just step around these, but in a scooter or wheelchair we simply couldn't get by them. On a crowded street we were trapped, which nearly put us off a kerb at one point. We also had to dodge people who just didn't see us because we were three feet lower than normal and out of their sight lines, so they whacked into the scooters.

David and I went our separate ways to find out whether Oxford was a wheelchair-friendly city. He took a very practical route – 'I decided to spend a penny and tried to access the disabled toilet in Market Street, the one highlighted in visitor information packs as being among the best, and located in the heart of the city. When I finally got there a car was parked about one foot away from the door and it was impossible to open. I couldn't get in at all. Then I went to a nearby department store, Boswells. There was limited space and I had tremendous difficulty getting into a lift. Behind me was this china display, with tureens, soup bowls, and twelve sets of plates, saucers and cups. I almost toppled it and, after ramming the thing gently a few times, I gave up on getting into that lift. I could just picture the headlines – Councillor Knocks Down China in Scooter. It helped me see the things disabled people have to put up with when they try to access what other people think of as normal services.'

I made a similar blunder when I arrived at the Golden Cross courtyard in central Oxford where Cranmer and Ridley had been imprisoned before being burned at the stake. I felt a distant kinship. A friend of mine owned a shop nearby called Plain Leather, so I went over to say hello. It was a struggle. After one small step up I had to take a sharp turn to the right. The shop was packed to the gills with belts and bags and suitcases. I did a tight tour of about ten feet and knocked four items to the floor.

I wanted to make my apology and scamper in my scooter, but that was impossible. I was caught in this little shop of leather horrors with buckles leering and straps hitting me. I felt so small because it all looked so tall. Fortunately it was all very soft and I didn't feel much when it was raining leather, but my exit was still slow and painful.

After that fiasco I needed a break, and besides it was freezing cold. Able-bodied people can walk up some heat. In a scooter the cold hits you hard. So I headed to the lap of luxury in Oxford city centre, the Randolph Hotel, which I knew had a fire in the foyer. It also had one set of stairs, not many – about three, but there might as well have been thirty. I would still have had the same problem, a complete impasse.

The staff were most helpful. The uniformed doorman, wearing a long military-style coat decorated with gold brocade, came out carrying a plank which he set up over the York stone stairs as a ramp. What fun. I backed out to the kerb for a bit of speed to tackle the 'lip' at the bottom and then slowly rode the ramp. I must have been five feet up, shivering at an awkward angle when I noticed that this particular plank didn't have any metal edges to guide the scooter wheels and prevent me from falling off.

It was not a wide plank so there was little margin for error. I froze, looked down at those steps with polished brass nosings and closed my eyes. This could be dangerous. It wouldn't be a soft landing if I fell and this two-hundred-pound metal scooter came crashing down on top of me. I inched my way up the ramp while a gaggle of people gathered to judge my progress.

I arrived safely to discover the end of the plank protruding over the landing and as I tried to come off the ramp the centre undercarriage of my four-wheel-drive scooter got stuck on the edge. I was beached. If this was going to be the pinnacle of my experience standing or sitting in the shoes of someone with a disability, it was the pits. I was slightly embarrassed. It wasn't so much the public humiliation, but the public display of being someone like Blanche DuBois who had 'always relied on the kindness of others'. I think it's all right to depend on the kindness of others, but why make it public? Some of the onlookers clambered up to lift the scooter and set me free, if that's the right word.

I headed for the fire, only to find a series of lounge chairs and tables blocking my way. By the time I finally reached the hot hearth I decided this tea time I would have a double gin and tonic.

Back at base, when I returned the scooter at the appointed time, Robin Brooks, head of this angelic Shopmobility scheme in a diabolic city, told me not everyone was so prompt. 'The husband of an American academic used to ride around Oxford on a scooter while his wife did research. One day he was a bit late back.

'This man didn't walk too well. Our vehicles can take a load up to thirty stone. He was close on that size, five feet six inches tall and weighed between twenty eight and twenty nine stone – a large gentleman, almost as wide as he was high.

'He decided to scoot along the towpath of the river Thames and rode to the Donnington Bridge where you can get to the path without using any steps, down a gravel incline which was rather steep. Most of our scooters can do a one in twelve gradient. This was probably one in six, the Thames Valley version of the Grand Canyon. A quarter of the way down, going lickety-split, he decided to call a halt and put the scooter into reverse. One of the shafts sheared in half and he went into freewheel – faster still.

'At the bottom of this gravel incline flowed the Thames. Shortly before entering this watery grave, the man bailed out by veering off sharply to the left into the nettles. Two of my mates at the Oxford Rowing Club across the river witnessed this and rang me to say, "One of your scooters is almost in the water."

'I found the large gentleman looking very dishevelled. He sat up in the nettles, disoriented and thanking his lucky stars that he wasn't floating face down in the river.'

I asked if they had ever lost a scooter to the river or the canals and waterways around Oxford, or indeed if they ever lost a customer. 'No scooters, but one customer – a man who came into the office when we first started. I do a five-second appraisal on people, summing them up and judging. Maybe I shouldn't, but I did an appraisal on him.

'He was in his mid-forties, looked like he needed feeding, very slim with long, mousey blond hair. He was just a normal guy, dressed rather like you and me in dark slacks and a shirt. Perhaps he was a bit dog-eared around the edges. I put that down to the fact that he might be living rough. I got this vibe right away that triggered something in me which said, "I really don't like you."

'He took one of the scooters and disappeared into the distance . . . and never came back. I cut him some slack, but an hour after closing time I went to St. Aldates police station and reported one of our vehicles missing.

'The Duty Officer looked surprised. "That's damn funny. We had one of them pulled up on the busiest road in the county, the A34, this afternoon. But he was not as you described him. Our officers stopped him going south on the northbound hard shoulder dressed in a pair of purple Y fronts and a ladies' blouse."

'Oh good, I said, you've got him. And the officer replied that no, they let him go.

'Those vehicles will do thirty-five miles on a full charge, and when the police questioned him he was already at one of the Abingdon turn-offs, a full nine miles away from Oxford city centre. We did get it back. Eventually we found the scooter just above Abingdon lock where the towpath changed sides, one of the two places where this happens. He was heading back to Oxford on the path, but our vehicles are not amphibious so he couldn't change to the other side of the canal. The driver just disappeared.

'We never did get to the bottom of this one – what motivates a customer to make things difficult . . . and what motivates people, shops, drivers and hotels in the city of Oxford to do the same.'

Chapter 18

A Hiding to Nothing
Sexual harassment at Oxford University.

Lift up the stones of Oxford University and some strange attitudes come crawling out.

One male don at Oxford argued that sexual harassment is positively desired, that there isn't a problem and that women quite enjoy it. Another don was so frightened about false accusations he refused to take tutorials with women students unless the door was propped open. A gay student told how his boyfriend was chased out of a formal dinner at his college, 'potatoes were thrown at him and he was hit with croquet mallets'.

Another undergraduate had a tutor who was venomously rude about her academic abilities. All her other tutors said she was doing well. After two terms of this man threatening to take her before the tutorial board for stupidity, she complained to her other college tutor, a woman, who indicated that 'he was known to have problems with women students, and she arranged for me to have another tutor. Everything is OK now but he made my time here a nightmare for my first two terms'.

In the 1990s attitudes toward sexual behaviour were in a state of flux, with many arguing that the University was shadow-boxing on this subject – if a member of faculty stepped out of line and chased undergraduates around the sofa, he could be promoted to a professorship and 'removed from temptation'. It has happened.

A survey of women in Oxford colleges by the Student Union indicated that 12% of the cases involved academic staff, while the vast majority, 42%, of the sexual harassing came from the women's male fellow students.

It was yet another example of an abuse of power, so I invited the University Senior Proctor, the top person in charge of behaviour and discipline, to discuss sexual harassment on air. Joanna Innes arrived in full battle dress. She was wearing subfusc – dark, formal clothes designed in the eighteenth century to be worn under the Oxford or Cambridge University gowns. As Proctor she had to wear those clothes day in and day out. They were her official uniform, but she could easily be mistaken for either a dominatrix or an ageing Jane Eyre. Two other dons followed in her wake: Susie Gibson, a lawyer, and philosopher Marianne Talbot.

'The Senior Proctor could easily be mistaken for either a dominatrix or an ageing Jane Eyre.'

Susie Gibson said she was taken aback by 'the level of sexual harassment which that survey seemed to indicate. I've taught at the University of Kent and Middlesex Poly, and I think I was aware of the amount of harassment which existed in those institutions, but I have to say that it wasn't a problem to the extent that the students have identified it in Oxford.'

The first problem was to define sexual harassment. According to the survey the group that suffered most as a result of this – straight, white women – emphasised the feelings of the recipient rather than the intent of the agent. So one don's compliment on a pretty face could be an undergraduate's sexual harassment.

The philosopher Marianne Talbot took a wider view: 'We're talking as if the only people who can be sexually harassed are women and of course that's false. I tried to persuade a colleague that I could quite easily harass a male student of mine and the reason I can do that or the way I can is that I have power over him. Harassment is a power game.'

And here her voice deepened. I wasn't sure if it was a female equivalent of Leslie Phillips or of Oliver Reed that was taking over.

'If I said to one of my students, "Well, that was a very good essay you wrote. In fact I'd like to discuss it a little more down at the pub." And at the pub I put my hand on his knee, perhaps in making a point on how good his essay was.

'Now would he really feel confident to say, "I'm sorry, I don't like what you're doing; I'm glad you like my essay but I don't like what you're doing"? Or would he think, Oh, dear, I have to put up with this or she's going to write a bad report on me?'

The lawyer agreed that sexual harassment can cut both ways. 'But with women there is something qualitatively different. Firstly they are more likely to get it and secondly because women see themselves as being constantly dealt with on the basis that they are sexual objects, they perceive this kind of harassment as a greater problem.

'When this happens to a male student, he doesn't have confirmed for him the sense that he is only a sexual object and that this is yet more of the way in which he's always perceived. I think for the male student who is subjected to sexual harassment that is unusual. It's out of step with the way in which he sees himself and his sense of what he is and who he is in the world. But when the object of sexual harassment is women, it's doubly destructive to them.'

If sexual harassment means different things to different people and is largely in the eye of the beholder, how do you deal with it? I knew from my own experience as a student that alcohol powers much of the social side of Oxford. Was this problem fuelled by alcohol? If it was, how do you solve that side of the equation?

Marianne Talbot agreed that alcohol was very much a part of the Establishment of Oxford. 'I was shocked the first time I went to a freshers dinner in Oxford. That is where the people who have just come up are introduced to college life. The amount that was allocated to each student was two sherries before dinner, three or four glasses of different wines with dinner and then something like port after dinner. You're looking there at eight or nine units of alcohol in one evening and that's from the Establishment. We give them that. It's hardly surprising that they think it's perfectly normal to consume eight, nine or ten units of alcohol a night at the pub.'

It seems that not much has changed over the years.

Susie Gibson, who could turn from a judge into a juror in an instant, agreed. 'We give it to them and we also drink it ourselves. In honesty one has to recognise that alcohol is a very major part of life in Oxford. I remember getting blind drunk as a student and I loved it . . . and we need to remember that when you're dealing with alcohol, it's not some evil that we can all agree has no benefits.'

Marianne Talbot put this in a moral context. 'You loved it. I know I did when I was young and first drinking, but I definitely had the feeling that if I was drinking to excess I wasn't doing the right thing. Whereas the impression we give in Oxford is that drinking to excess is perfectly acceptable behaviour.'

The Senior Proctor Joanna Innes helped paint the picture. 'Sometimes what we are talking about is drunken undergraduates hanging around in college bars, groping or yelling at women who come into the bar in a way that even the same people sober might well agree is not a very reasonable way to behave.'

Consider this 'name and address supplied' story of alcohol and sex in another Student Union survey that goes beyond harassment. 'A fellow fresher spiked my drinks when we visited another college bar together, then came up to my room on our return (uninvited), would not leave when asked, and raped me.

'Subsequently he visited my room several other times, when he tried to become intimate with me and also became violent. On most of these occasions he was drunk. The most frightening incident, apart from the rape itself, was when he tried to force me to go up to his room, and when I ran up to my boyfriend's room, he chased me right across the quad. I was terrified.

'I reported all this two terms afterwards. In the end College said they could not make a judgement on what happened as (surprise, surprise) there were no witnesses, and the boy's version of events was very convincing. They refused to take into account the fact that he was an alcoholic, drug addict and had been violent on other occasions (not in a sexual context). They cautioned me that I was not allowed to tell anyone about what had happened as it might cause the boy problems.'

Since most of the sexual harassment comes from the women's fellow students, 42%, I thought it strange that the University tutors focused mainly on the relationship between staff and students and not on the bigger problem of what goes on between students.

The lawyer, Susie Gibson, made a fine distinction here. 'The fact that only 12% of perceived sexual harassment has come from tutors isn't to make that a minor problem because the impact that such harassment from tutors can have on students is phenomenal. One can't get too tied up in terms of the quantity of sexual harassment. I think one has to consider the quality of sexual harassment, if one can put it that way. It is by no means a minor problem.'

The Senior Proctor explained: 'It's not that students don't make each other uncomfortable, but there is an issue of principle about whether it's appropriate for university or college authorities to intervene in what many people regard as students' private lives.

'It's quite commonly said that in the 1970s the University decided to start treating students as adults and leave them to organise their own affairs, and the argument about what to do in this area is not an argument about whether it's a serious problem, but what is an appropriate and effective intervention.'

Susie Gibson touched on the legal aspects of enforcement and agreed that the alcohol factor and students harassing each other are 'very serious problems but in what way can the college or university authorities set about policing undergraduate behaviour, if I can use a slightly awkward word like policing? I think there is a sense that none of us wants to be acting as substitute parents and policing student behaviour in a way that suggests they are not fully mature.'

Sexual harassment was a pressing and important problem and mainly among the students, but the three dons discussing this obviously wanted to focus on it from the point of view of academic staff. The Senior Proctor: 'I would distinguish between cases which clearly involve relationships of authority from cases that involve people whose relationships are social or informal. I think in the case of members of staff the university might well want to say certain sorts of behaviour are inappropriate and we don't countenance them, even if the person harassed in the end thinks she's prepared to put up with it and doesn't go ahead with the complaint.

'But it's the case of how we police students that the question of where we draw the line and how we become engaged is most problematic.'

The question remains. Does Oxford University have dual standards here, one for the staff and another for the students? Why are dons prepared to police the actions of other dons even when the victim has withdrawn her complaint and yet shy away from using the same robust approach of policing the behaviour of those students who are sexually harassing 'their equals'?

The last word goes to the lawyer who didn't exactly grasp the nettle. 'I think we have to remember that these students are eighteen when they come up and twenty-one at graduation, and many of the graduate students are older than that. They're young adults old enough to vote, to go to war. I think there is a moral difficulty in attempting to continue to treat young people as if they were still living at home and telling them 'you're not young adults, you're really children'. I think it's a very difficult line to tread. If we allow ourselves to get into a position of issuing directives about behaviour which don't acknowledge that these are young people who have to learn to be autonomous, then we get ourselves onto a hiding to nothing.'

Chapter 19

Simple, Cheerful and Enjoyable
Funerals can be fun

Is BBC local radio 'God's Waiting Room', where listeners are on their last legs, stuck in the past, afraid of the future and about to die? Two listeners, Barbara and David Huelin, raised that question when they rang to invite me to visit them and view their coffins.

They were in robust health when I arrived and gave me a glass of Rioja, Gran Reserva 1989, to get me in the mood. What mood do I need? I thought. After a bottle in their garden beside the Oxford canal, I took the plunge, inspected the caskets and invited them on my programme to convince me that funerals can be fun.

Barbara painted the picture on air. 'It all started with an article and photo in *The Guardian*, very pleasant sunny picture of a hardware store in Gainsborough, with some coffins leaning up against the front window. Underneath was a sign saying "Chipboard covered in Fablon" – good old veneer Fablon – "£56." Just the ticket, I thought.

'So I rang the man to place an order. He asked me to send the measurements and said, "Don't forget to send me your hips. The hips are very important." I sent him the information, but didn't hear anything. Six months later I phoned again. He sucked his teeth and said, "Very sorry, but my source has dried up. I'm having difficulty in obtaining any more coffins." I thought that's funny because that's his trade, but then I realised his trade is to sell screwdrivers and planes and dustbins – hardware. I think he was a new boy on the block in the idea of selling coffins to the public. Jolly good idea too.

'It's not easy to get a good coffin off the hook. I've read about a woman who discussed her husband's death. She wrote to Sainsbury's – don't they run that DIY store called Homebase? – and suggested they ought to have coffins for sale – cash and carry – but she got a cool response from Sainsbury's who didn't think it would set the right kind of . . . tone.

'My chap in Gainsborough was frightfully sorry but emphatic– no more coffins. I suppose coffins are usually manufactured and sold to funeral undertakers and it's not really usual for everyday people, the customers, to break in on that monopoly.

'So I got on my bike that autumn and went around visiting local undertakers in Oxford. I said that I'd like to make an enquiry, and they took that in their stride. "Oh yes, do come in . . . and what sort of a funeral were you requiring?" or "who's died?" You know – nice questions but I said, "No, actually it isn't that. I want to buy a coffin", and they thought that was a little unusual or even possibly . . . unnatural. Then I added, "Well, actually, two." They said, "Oh" and then they looked me up and down and told me I really didn't need to bother myself because I looked as though I had another twenty years good life in me.

'I didn't get much joy. It was a package deal, the whole works or nothing – certainly no coffin on its own.

'There was one rather revealing occasion at an undertaker's where the manager said – he'd been sent for because it was a rather peculiar request I'd made – he said, "Well there's warpage."

'"I beg your pardon?"

'"Well there's warpage."

'"Oh do explain more," I urged.

'"You see you can't really store them because the lid might warp," which I thought was a bit strange. They must do a kind of quick turnover in these coffins that come down from the factories on a sort of conveyer belt. Anyway that was all no go.'

'Warpage– that's a lovely one! Are you sure they weren't talking about your mind?' I asked.

'Oh probably,' Barbara said lightly. 'You know Oxford is full of loony North Oxford ladies, and I'm one of them. I got home and said to David, "I won't have it. This is abominable. They are straight-arming me on the coffin front. Look here, you've got to build these coffins yourself."'

'That's right,' agreed David, 'and since I slightly pride myself on being something of a handy man I agreed and built two coffins – one for each of us. And they both fit, we've tried them on.'

'I was quite impressed by the little details, like the headrests. What made you think of that?' I asked.

Barbara and David Huelin, two of the most dead pan funeral arrangers I've ever met.

David said, 'A really nice tip from the only helpful undertaker we met, one out of four or five. He told us we'd have to have a cushion or something, because "if you put a dead body down flat the head falls back and it doesn't look good". So I put in those little platforms for our heads to rest on, and if Barbara wants to put in a few cushions of dried herbs or something, well, that will make it all the better.'

'And the lids,' I pointed out, 'aren't you afraid they're going to warp?'

'Oh, no, I don't think so; I chose blockboard to make my coffins. It's lighter than chipboard and easier to work, and it doesn't warp because the grain crosses over and over. It's a bit like plywood but not so heavy so it won't warp, but even if it does, I've provided for screws all the way round the edge of the lid. Each coffin has its little box inside that says 'screws' on the top. And our friend the joiner next door has offered to come around with his screwdriver when he's needed. And he's also going to save up some cedar-wood shavings, because you would rattle around a bit in our coffins since we don't have any of this pleated satin sort of stuff inside. It's just plain wood, so the cedar shavings would be a nice mattress, so to speak, and they will smell quite beautiful.

'We're very happy with the handles because we managed to get away from those dreadful brass or plastic jobs. I decided that what we really needed was rope of some sort. We went to the boatyard in Abingdon and the chandler produced a beautiful soft-textured nylon mooring rope of half-an-inch diameter. It was just the job because since it was nylon you could melt it on the inside and anchor it to the coffin wood with a steel or brass washer. It looks nice, it's easy to handle and it costs almost nothing into the bargain.'

'We worked out that each coffin costs just under fifty pounds,' explained Barbara. 'I mean, of course, there is no labour charge because David is the carpenter. But if someone wants to knock up a coffin the labour shouldn't be much. And we bought some emulsion to paint them dark green. I thought I would like to have some flowers on the lid of my coffin and I asked my good friend and artist Kassandra if she would like to paint some poppies on the lid, which is not going to warp, and she's just finished.'

'It did strike me that these coffins have something of the feel of the houseboats on the Oxford canal,' I ventured. 'Were you aiming for that?'

Barbara again, 'Well, we are living beside the canal and that's where we plotted and hatched this scheme, so perhaps we did get some inspiration from the canal boats. After all we are going on a journey.'

David – 'We did plot and hatch and we wanted to be somewhat discreet about it all, but that proved difficult. We had two rather noisy afternoons sawing up the wood in the yard so we had to alert the neighbours. Then I took the materials down to the canalside where I have my workshop and started putting them together. That's where Barbara's friends began to see me making coffins and wondered if she was all right.'

Barbara – 'A few days later I was on one of the Oxford buses going into town when my friend Gwen boarded and said, "Well, HELLO, Barbara!" in a slightly profuse manner. I like Gwen and she likes me, but not that much. "I'm so glad to see you!" she gushed. "I was very worried I hadn't seen you for some time. You know I walk up and down the towpath and I thought I saw your husband . . ." Oh, you must mean the coffins David's making. The bus was full of people and everyone turned around. It took a while for the idea to sink in. "Well," Gwen said, "I hadn't seen you about . . ."'

'You've had a lot of fun, but basically it's a very serious thing you are doing. It comes down to how you view life, death and your family,' I suggested.

Barbara – 'This whole procedure – the arrangement of our funerals and how we left our belongings – is something that we've done together; and I feel certain that when the first of us pops off the other is going to have rather good feelings about everything that is about to happen because we arranged it together.'

David – 'There is an element of continuity. If there is any life after death it is there in the recollections of the surviving member of a partnership and the family, and that was the principal good outcome of this strangely absorbing interest that we have developed. Another point that emerges is that thinking about death and preparing for it and preparing for the disposal of one's remains doesn't, apparently, bring death any nearer, and failing to think about it doesn't prevent it happening, apparently. Our son is a vicar, and I think he has seen that a lot of his parishioners for one reason or another have not had the opportunity or the idea to face up to these things. He was quite pleased that we had and he fell in with our ideas. So did our girls. They didn't think we were "barmy old mum and dad".'

'What about your friends who might not be wishing to think about these things?' I wanted to know if they had started any hares running in their circles.

Barbara – 'Well, I believe that quite a few of them have begun to think about all that's involved. One thing does lead to another. Before we built the coffins we had always wanted to be cremated because we thought it was clean, neat and easy, the sensible thing, less trouble and more ecological, a very green idea. We thought we had better go to the crem and check to see what kind of coffin they would accept. It's no use arriving at the front door and being turned away because your coffin doesn't comply. So we roped in Ingrid to help us, and she entered into the spirit of all this and drove us to the crem because I use a bicycle only and it's a long way and David doesn't ride anymore. Anyway, Ingrid has told all her friends.'

David – 'And if there is one thing positive that comes from all this fanfare it will be that we might have inspired a number of people to think about this question rather more seriously than most people do. If you think about it and make your arrangements before-hand, the whole thing loses its terror.

'When people are bereaved suddenly they are mentally and emotionally upset and not necessarily able to make sensible, sound judgements. They are an easy victim and prey for unscrupulous operators, not that there are any, but . . . it's a particularly vulnerable time in one's life.'

Barbara – 'At the crem we met the manager who told us what sort of coffin he would accept. It had to be combustible and it should not have too many metal parts and no plastic lining, so what we had planned conformed to what they require and we passed the 'coffin test'. But he passed the 'ashes test'. I hadn't had a lot of experience at crems and I wanted to know what actually happens once the body is lowered or shunted on rails when the curtain closes. After that we don't know what happens, and I wanted to know – did one really receive at the end the ashes of the loved one.'

'Nobody asks that sort of question, Barbara,' I ventured.

Barbara – 'Well, I wanted to know. And he was absolutely specific about this – they would definitely be David's ashes or my ashes and nobody else's because of the way his ovens were constructed, which he explained to us, and how things are riddled through and then at the bottom there is a pile of ash. It's pulled to one side and cooled down, and you come back in 24 hours and you can have them in an urn. He did say, also, that they could be delivered to you via Securicor, if you wanted.'

David – 'But something happened at the end of our interview. We had a good walk in the rose gardens and we thought we could smell a lot of carbon monoxide because the furnace was on and doing its work and we were up behind the building and not much lower than the chimney. We were able to see the hot gas rising out of the chimney. You know how it hazes. There was a strong smell of burning gas, and it suddenly dawned on us that some significant atmospheric pollution was going on here. Everyone cremated pollutes the atmosphere. So that rather put us off the idea. And the act of cremation, reducing a body to ashes, also reduces the personal element that we were talking about earlier, the personal relationship that subsists between the dead one and the survivors which lasts for quite a time. It seems to cut that off, this continuity of family feeling.'

Barbara – 'On the subject of pollution, we noticed that since then there are now very strict new laws about cremation. But we gave up on the idea of the big fire and went home and thought about a burial. In the forty years we have been married we are great ones for having huge discussions while washing up. David washes and I dry and we discuss the funeral or whatever it is.

'We went to Wolvercote cemetery in Oxford and were greeted by the deputy superintendent, Janet Simmonds, and the atmosphere was fantastic. You just felt like you had come home. They were so understanding and interested in what we were doing. They even liked the idea that the arrival at the cemetery would be in a friend's car or van, any old van would do. We will not have a shiny hearse. She was delighted with all this.

'She had recently helped a family bury someone who was also a member of a jazz band and the band came along too and did their stuff. It's wonderful . . . so releasing, isn't it? I don't think people often go there ahead, like we did, it's probably unusual, but we felt a kindred spirit in her.'

David – 'We've got a double-decker plot, where we would be stacked one on top of the other, and you can get that for £120 in this municipal cemetery, a ten-star place. We've bought it and I have the title deeds to prove it.

'When the time comes, we have two teams of six each to carry the coffin. That's not really gilding the lily. People might not feel like it on the day or maybe they will have popped off themselves, you never know. We wrote to all our friends and asked and they said they would like to do it.'

Barbara – 'The chapel of rest place will be in our house, good old-fashioned stuff. Then we'll put the lid on. We have thirty-six screw holes, because it looks nice and of course that's to combat warpage . . . They are small screws, so you need a certain number to keep the lid firmly down.

'And when we arrive at the cemetery I know that Janet or her boss Hugh will be there to welcome us, and we'll be so happy to be in a place where we are greeted by people we know. They will have arranged for the grave digger. We've met him; he's a delightful man, a good sort of countryman, basic Oxford type. We asked him if he would be digging for us and he said, yes, he would and was looking forward to the day, so to speak.'

David – 'It should be a celebration of someone's life. I hope this will give our children something to remember, loving and cheerful. If you have been to an opera, you applaud if it was any good. When I die it will be the end of that opera and if people want to applaud, jolly good. If they don't, well, too bad, I shan't be worried; but the end of someone's life is like the end of a performance and you applaud it.'

Bill – 'I just think that when people do go to funerals and they are confronted with the gleaming black casket and hearse and the shiny-shoed men standing around, there is something that is distinctly sad and impersonal about it all. You've managed to avoid that.'

Barbara – 'There is something very important about a funeral and the grieving that goes with it, and I just think the family should be involved in this process and if they are, it will make the grieving more meaningful to everyone involved. It took me twenty years to grieve for my mother's death, and I would like that to be avoided for my children.'

Bill – 'It strikes me that what you are giving by your funeral – and most people don't 'give' things by their funeral because things are done unto people – but what you are doing is giving to your family a very special gift.'

David – 'In a way, yes, I think what we are trying to do is to make matters simple, cheerful and enjoyable, despite the fact that maybe we shall be missed. But what we are doing, now, almost unconsciously, is to create an occasion that they will enjoy and remember for the rest of their lives as not altogether sad.

'And if in the process other people latch onto this idea and if they can in turn give something to their families and can make their departure bearable for the survivors, well so much the better. We will feel, if we survive to see it happen, that we have done a little bit of good in this wicked world. And we did it all for well under four hundred pounds, and that's including the Champagne . . .'

Barbara – 'What? Oh, David, we haven't even discussed the Champagne yet. Whatever next!'

A typical conversation in 'God's Waiting Room'?

Chapter 20

How Does Oxford Taste?

Raymond Blanc and the cost of cabbage.

Food is a subject that divides Oxford, even in the colleges of Oxford University where undergraduates may suffer inexcusable meals while the dons dine at high table in the same hall in some splendour. I asked a local luminary in the food firmament to take a culinary snapshot of Oxford at the end of the twentieth century and find out whether or not the Brits had any taste in matters of taste.

Raymond Blanc, chef of some skill and the brains behind the hotel and Michelin-starred restaurant Le Manoir aux Quat' Saisons in Oxfordshire, told me, 'I came to England in 1972 and I must say it was like coming into the asshole of the food world . . . OK, I chose the wrong word. Let's put it this way, it was the best worst food in the whole of Europe. It was a time when the tin opener was the most important gadget to have in a kitchen, where to be a chef you had to have a frontal lobotomy. You had to be a total failure, basically a social outcast, to be a chef.

'A manager had to be equally an outcast with the worst possible "A" levels so that any decent university would not dream of taking him. And the waiters didn't know better either because the people who qualified to be waiters were the people who couldn't qualify to be a chef. OK, that means those guys were subservient and basically had no pride and no joy in a job well done.

'So this industry was in total decay and the consumers didn't know better. They loved these piles of bad food on their plates. And the farmers were just as horrible. British farmers invented intensive farming, which standardised all the produce. You had animals that were not worth eating, like these horrible ducks that were full of fat. The chain food was horrendous as well.

'The food industry, the service and the food production were all a total disaster. But within twenty years we are privileged to have food that is very special. We are talking about a revolution, a food revolution that has conquered this country.'

I turned to Janet Thorne, a senior lecturer in nutrition at Oxford Brookes University, wanting to know why British food has been poor in the past and why the British didn't have any sense of quality.

Her reply was thoughtful. 'I think it's a post-war problem. People didn't have enough money to spend on food, the cost of living went up, petrol went up, and people were not willing to spend the money on food. But in the last fifteen years there's been this huge foodie revolution and great interest in cooking at home. Magazines wall to wall . . . I've got six metres of cookery books at home. I'm as bad as everyone else, but they are almost pornography – you know, you read them, you don't necessarily do them. One only cooks at the weekends, that sort of thing.'

Raymond Blanc had been looking at his hands and touching the tips of his fingers together. He stopped, clasped his hands, looked over to Janet and raised his eyebrows: 'Interesting lady here . . .'

Janet was flirting with him. 'I'll see you later, Raymond . . . The British diet is awful. We have almost the worst diet in the world as far as health is concerned, even now. Our intake of vegetables is going down, and it's the same with bread. Cheese consumption is on the skids. People are eating other things. They're buying rubbish – crisps, burgers and made-up food. Go around the supermarkets; they are a handy guide to what people are eating. Look at how many metres are devoted to junk foods. The Brits don't care about food in their souls the way French people do.'

Raymond Blanc agreed that it's down to the British culture and to change culture will take some time. 'But what we are witnessing now is absolutely wonderful. Food is on television, in books, all over the place. You attack supermarkets but I think that is a bit unfair, they have led the revolution. Fifteen years ago try to find fresh tarragon or fresh basil . . . but today you can find all this and the Asian spices and varieties. British supermarkets are now adventurous, better than the French.'

When I go into a supermarket I see tomatoes with a label boasting that they are grown for flavour, so I asked if they knew what's going wrong with the food supply if this fundamental attribute is offered as an optional extra to boast about.

Raymond Blanc thought that was general everywhere. 'In the USA, Britain or France, and it's all down to the shame of agriculture. It's all intensive. These huge operators are controlled by money. They are not interested in flavour; they are interested in yield.'

I suggested that attitudes to food also owe something to the class system. 'There are certain people who don't know about food and don't care and eat lousy food.'

Janet Thorne admitted: 'I have students at Oxford Brookes University who have no idea how to cook and this is evident in the classes especially with white males. People who are very poor cannot afford to buy extremely expensive foods, so they are probably buying poor quality, poor value-for-money foods. They buy crisps and bottles of lemonade, and a package of crisps is a very expensive way of buying half a potato that's been murdered.'

Raymond Blanc drew on his childhood experiences to argue for more creativity with food: 'My mother — I come from very much a working-class family — and my mother had such a small budget to feed five children, and yet she could manage to create the most wholesome food. Yes, perhaps she would spend half of her day at the stove, which of course a modern man or woman cannot do anymore. But on the other hand, now we just need to discover a little bit of the old-fashioned creativity and imagination.

'It is so satisfying to create something delicious and healthy and give it to your kids. We have forgotten completely what food means, not only in terms of sensuality, but in terms of sharing it, sitting around a table, being able to talk to each other. That's the kind of food culture we need.

'We live in a society that is dangerously too fast; it's all convenience now. We eat from a little plastic bag that we shove in the microwave. We give that to our kids and think it is an act of love . . . it's an act of hate.

'Class does play a part in how we look at food. A very large segment of the population is working class, and they are not only ignorant about food, but also prejudiced against quality. They are prejudiced against going into a good restaurant to spend money. They think it is wasted money. A burger is fine, but they think it is immoral to spend money on good food.'

I pointed out a slight problem with his view: 'You say people should go out and spend lots of money on this food, well, what if they don't have the money? They simply might not be able to afford it.'

Raymond Blanc: 'Nonsense. You don't have to have much money. You can cook a good meal for one pound. Give me a pound and you'll see what I can do with that!'

Bill: 'Fine, what could you cook for one pound?'

Raymond Blanc: 'OK, top of my mind . . . give me two leeks, a piece of ham, lait béchamel instead of cream, a bit of grated cheese on the top and you have the most wholesome dish that you bake in the oven. It will take you two minutes' work. It's not time-consuming, but you need to know a little bit about what you are doing. It's simple enough. Money and time are not excuses any more, and if you give me two pounds I will give you fabulous food.'

At current prices a typical meal for two without wine on the modestly priced — not to say cheaper — menu at Raymond Blanc's restaurant, Le Manoir aux Quat' Saisons, would cost £219.00.

Chapter 21

A Polite Picture
Echoes in Oxford of the Rwandan genocide

In broadcasting a little bit of fear goes a long way. People can smell it over the airwaves. Fear has a habit of slipping over words and curdling them; so something fresh could sound stale, something honest could stink. I didn't think this would be a problem when I interviewed the man who had stood up to mass murderers during the Rwandan genocide. A man in that position had to be fearless or he had to be dead.

Paul Rusesabagina, the former general manager of the Mille Collines, a luxury hotel in Kigali, was promoting his book *An Ordinary Man – the true story behind the film 'Hotel Rwanda'*. I agreed to host a public debate with Paul in central Oxford and he agreed to an extended interview on air.

Paul was outwardly undistinguished, not of great stature, his cheekbones a bit padded, his eyes bright and darting over a thick nose

with slightly fanned nostrils, a trimmed moustache hovered over round large lips that often broke into a ready smile. He was a quiet, gentle man, easily overlooked. In short he was a Hutu, part of the majority group in Rwanda who held the reins of power and who slaughtered the Tutsis in the genocide.

As a Hutu who was protecting the Tutsis he had a unique perspective on the slaughter, so I asked him to describe the beginning of that nightmare.

'In April 1994 when Rwanda went insane and mass murderers swept over the country, 800,000 people were butchered in 100 days by their friends and neighbours. I hid 1,268 people inside the Mille Collines. I knew my hotel could become an abattoir at any time.

'The genocide sprang from racial hatred. Most of the people hiding in my hotel were Tutsis, the descendants of the former ruling class of Rwanda. The people who wanted to kill them were the traditional farmers, generally Hutus.

'There is supposed to be a visual difference between them. Tutsis are tall and thin with delicate noses. Hutus are supposed to be short and dumpy with wider noses. These two groups had been living together

Paul Rusesabagina, the man whose story reached the world through the film 'Hotel Rwanda'.

for half a millennium in an uneasy relationship. Several had crossed over to the other side like I had: my mother was a Tutsi and so was my wife.

'On day one of the genocide doctors were dragged from their homes and shot at point blank range in the face. Old women had their throats slit. The murderers whacked schoolchildren with wooden planks and then cracked open their skulls under their boot heels. They threw elderly people down the holes of outhouses and buried them under buckets of rocks.

'Thousands died that day. But throughout the next one hundred days the Mille Collines was one of the few places in Kigali where nobody was killed.'

I knew that the murderers had cut off electricity and stopped water reaching the Mille Collines after a few weeks, so at night over a thousand refugees had to live in shadows and darkness. I wondered how he dealt with that.

'Well, at first I began to use a generator, but that broke down and we stayed in total darkness. I had to start cutting down trees in the hotel grounds for fire. Our food was limited to corn and dry beans. You can never understand how it is to have over a thousand people looking at you for a meal. It was complicated.'

The loss of electricity was a psychological tactic by the murderers to intimidate Paul and his people, but at worst it was only an inconvenience. The lack of water was more serious. That could be a killer, making people choose between staying at the hotel and dying of dehydration or dying on the streets if they left the hotel. I wanted to know how he got around that threat.

As always he was pragmatic in his response. 'We had reserve water tanks under the basement which I checked several times each day and saw their levels plummeting and I knew we would not get any fresh deliveries; so I turned the swimming pool into a tool of life. It had about 78,000 gallons of water and we put a rationing system in place to share out the water equally.

'This ordinary-looking pool used to be called the shadow capital of Rwanda because it was here that local power brokers did deals with aid donors, arms dealers and World Bank officials. Now it was a place where the powerless got a longer lease on life.'

I knew he had done a bit of multi-tasking during the 100 days of the genocide. He had this flock of over a thousand traumatised people inside the hotel, where three times every day he had to find enough loaves and fishes to fight off famine, and fix the plumbing and keep spirits up. At the same time he was reaching out to people in the streets who were being slaughtered and helping them escape to the relative safety of the Mille Collines. Then he found a hidden phone line and faxed the White House, the UN, and the Quai d'Orsay, whoever he thought might listen. I asked how difficult it was to keep all of those balls in the air at the same time.

'Yes . . . it had its moments, and at the same time I was welcoming killers, the soldiers, into the hotel. I welcomed the militia men because if you want to control someone you have to keep them close, and share a drink with them and sit around the table and talk. Many times at the end of my dialogue with the murderers I would give them a cask of good wine or champagne. I knew it would be confiscated in the end, so why should I not use it to prolong that end?'

And yet on each of those 100 days of the genocide, he could have been killed at any time. I wanted to understand what kind of a lease on life he thought he had.

'Well, I was no more afraid to be killed. I was sure to be killed. By whom, where, how was he going to do it – those were a few questions I was asking myself. At a particular point in all this it was clear that before they could kill the refugees they would have to kill me; so I had condemned myself to death.

'I kept a little money back in the hotel safe. That was for me to give one last bribe so they would kill me with a bullet rather than hack us apart with machetes. Our project was not to die, but to die a better death, and to die with a bullet was a better death. We did not want to be tortured.'

Where do I go from here . . . we were near the end of the interview, so I asked him if all this had shaken his faith in humanity a bit.

'Yes, it has shifted everything. Before the genocide I believed that people were reasonable, trustworthy. Now I have changed all that.'

Bill: 'Your book gave me nightmares.'

Paul: 'Oh, it is quite light, compared with what happened this is a polite picture.'

After the radio interview I drove us into central Oxford where Paul was scheduled to have a public question and answer session with me on stage at the Museum of Natural History. During the short journey Paul was in a reflective mood, maybe because we had just come out of a radio studio, a safe and supportive place and now we were headed into a public place.

He started talking where our programme had ended: the subject of his death. 'You know, I left Rwanda because I thought I might be killed there, so I've come to a safe country . . . but I know it's not safe, and I know I'll never be safe . . . entirely.'

We were late, but everyone knew this would be the case because the radio programme ended shortly before the scheduled public debate was due to start. We ran up to the huge wooden doors of this Victorian museum which were closed and discovered they were locked.

Paul dug out the instructions from his publisher which said yes, this was the right venue; so we banged on the metal knocker. After a slight pause the neo-gothic doors opened a crack, so someone could size us up. There was a bit of a flurry and we could hear the creak of these 19th century hinges opening just enough for us to slip through. Inside we were bundled up to the lecture theatre and escorted into the wings from a side door and began the public performance.

Sometimes when alarm bells should ring, they don't. Neither Paul nor I took note of the small fact that the entrance to a public building for a public event was locked. We didn't know that 'a Rwandan group' had sent a letter to the Oxford venue saying something like 'Are you aware this man has spread falsehoods?'. The publishers wanted adequate security so two men stood at the door checking everyone's tickets.

Twenty minutes before the performance five people turned up and only three had tickets. They said friends who were in the theatre had their tickets, and they demanded entry. These people were from Rwanda and had driven to Oxford from Birmingham for this event and they were going inside. The door staff did not back down but later told me, 'You could see the machetes in their eyes. One man who appeared to be the leader was smartly dressed. He was older and took charge. There was a glare in his eyes that gave me a chilling feeling. His eyes were big and he was trying to intimidate us by saying, "Let us in or something might happen".'

Paul and I walked out on stage and sat down a few feet from the audience; the stage was just a raised platform three feet above the level of the front row seats. We unfolded the story of the genocide and the role of the Mille Collines hotel much as we had done earlier on air, and opened the floor to questions.

It was a packed auditorium, all white except for a group of black people who sat very near the front in the centre. They were visibly unimpressed by the proceedings and several raised their hands to ask Paul a question.

Their contribution was not so much a question as a statement of accusations against Paul, saying he was seen as an outcast in Rwanda; he was lying; he was an enemy of the state. I asked them to put their view into the form of a question. They ignored me. I repeated my request.

By this time they were standing up, shouting and pointing. Later the security man told me at that stage he had a feeling that something might 'kick off'.

I've done several of these Q and A sessions, so it was easy for me to shift the focus from this group to other questioners. When they persisted, I was able to reinforce the fact that they had had their time and they were now finished. It was simply a case of enlisting the energy, attention and authority of the audience to stop anything happening.

The event ended shortly after that, and Paul and I walked off stage together, now separated completely from the audience. As we reached the wings and left the limelight, he reached over to me and I could see, for the first time the fear that perhaps had been lurking there all the time we were together. Then he whispered to me in a low voice without a trace of irony, 'Thank you, thank you for saving me.'

Chapter 22

Smoothing out the Social Wrinkles
The discreet charm of the North Oxford bourgeoisie.

Interviewing people on local radio can expand your social circle in the most unexpected manner. On the national networks most of the contributors are hired mouths, professional spin doctors, experts and people-in-suits. At the local level, guests tend to be real people who are accidentally caught up in the limelight or who feel passionately about the big and small issues of the day – the war on terrorism, Iran, the war on the rat population in Oxford.

Shamin was one of my guests whom I probably never would have met off-air. She came to Great Britain from Iran over thirty years ago and set up her own very successful business in Oxford. After the radio interview we kept in contact and she invited me to a dinner with a difference.

The discreet charm of the bourgeoisie in North Oxford was put to the test when two women who do ironing for twenty-four of them turned the tables and invited their clients to a dinner party.

The ironers hired a Lebanese restaurant, Al Shami, for a five-course meal, including bottles of Chateau Musar 1989 – a menu considered too expensive for the Christmas party of my colleagues at the BBC, who opted instead for the cheaper fare at the Randolph Hotel of Inspector Morse fame in central Oxford.

By eight o'clock the guests had arrived, at sixes and sevens because they had no connection with each other except through one channel: each regularly handed over his or her laundry to the hosts, and these now stood at the door holding out their arms in welcome – Shamin in a basic black dress with a diaphanous gold shawl and Jousf in an immaculate red sari.

We have all been to dinners with strangers before – charity galas, business lunches, political fundraisers – where buyers and sellers were held together by an economic thread. This was different.

Would the practical people of North Oxford be slightly ashamed to be celebrating the fact that they didn't do their own ironing, when they knew very well they could or should be doing it?

Or would they be speculating, secretly, on just how lucrative is this business of ironing? Was the new kind of gentry edgy because the new kind of servant was inviting them out to dinner; and if one went, what was one's model for behaviour? Was there any life left in the old master/servant relationship? And by the way, which was which nowadays?

The guests exuded the appearance of people who were looked after – no creases, not too many cares, a lot of cold cream, charming – but they didn't look completely comfortable.

'It was that kind of dinner party. People crossed knives and forks, lines and purposes.'

The question lurking behind their half-smiles was fundamental: who are all these other people, why did they come, and what can I possibly have in common with them?

In this room full of people with four-by-fours who might drive their children 200 yards to school, I bumped into the only one who couldn't drive. Twirling the silver handle of her walking stick with the same dexterity that she swirled her wine, a woman in a well-ironed black dress with pearl necklaces down to her knees introduced herself as Patricia and began to explain how she became lame.

'During the Raj, when I was a nine-year-old girl in the Bombay hospital of Lady Windlesham, I suffered an attack of arthritic paralysis. I lay there unable to move and thinking I must be letting down the whole British Empire.' Shamin approached and embraced us both. 'Bill, I'm so glad you've met Lady Moss.'

India and the Raj came to life, as did Oxford. Patricia said she was known as the Duchess of Osney, 'and the people on the island who call me that don't necessarily say it with sweetness.'

The ice was slowly breaking for me, but the next guest I met shook it violently. This punk-like Presbyterian from Scotland dropped a fairly heavy hint that he used to sell pornography in his student days but now teaches maths at one of the most expensive public schools in the country.

I had assumed it would be difficult for the other guests to measure up to these two, but Carola turned out to be a sex therapist from Italy, and we had a most informative discussion about impotence and vaginismus.

It was that kind of dinner party. People crossed knives and forks, lines and purposes. There were no roles, rules or restrictions, so I took the opportunity to ask everyone: 'Why are we all here?'

The silence that greeted my question told me that, yes, there was still a line and I had crossed it. But then I didn't start on the same side of the line as everyone else. I was the only guest who was not a client. I do my own ironing – at least twice a year. Shamin and I had met in a BBC studio when I interviewed her and we liked each other. I was a guest because I was a friend. What were the others?

'I'm here because Shamin and Jousf do my ironing,' said a management consultant at Unipart, but she left a question hanging in the air by that answer. It was curt, clinical and clearly no reason by itself to draw her into a dinner party unless she was being extremely patronising, which she wasn't.

There was a further silence.

The sex therapist jumped in. 'This isn't something that I have to think about, analyse or justify. I feel like I belong here; and if you need to know why, the answer is that I admire Shamin.'

'For what, for doing your chores?' I asked.

'No, because I know her and the two boys and her daughter, and somehow as with each of my friends, we became connected. We can't shrug that off. It's something to celebrate, almost against the odds. I don't like to mention it since it seems so obvious, but we're just simply equals.'

An aggressive Chinese woman was suddenly slow and measured. 'Shamin and Jousf are ordinary women who do things with dignity, even – that's right – even ironing.

'The fact that they do this chore, as you call it, the ironing, helps keep us both in balance and allows us a little opportunity to be free, each in our own way. I need this particular freedom, and so do they. But with Shamin and Jousf we are not just free, we are friends.'

It was a dinner party with right-on smells and bells, but did they really mean it? The true test is – would they do it again? The sex therapist broke into my thoughts, took our names and telephone numbers and promised that next month she would whip us up a mean zabaglione.

Tony Martin on my programme shortly after his release from prison.

Chapter 23

'Straw Dogs' comes to Oxford
Protecting a farm that's under attack.

If your home were under attack, how far would you go to protect your family or property? Would you reach for a gun, and could you pull the trigger? These questions came to the boil in a heated debate after Norfolk farmer Tony Martin shot dead an intruder in the middle of the night at his remote farmhouse at Emneth Hungate. He was sentenced to three years for manslaughter. Tony was a guest on my programme and our discussion disturbed some buried memories in one listener.

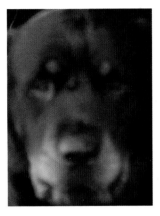

Colin rang me after the programme. His voice was shaky and he sounded a little out of breath. 'I've aimed a gun at an attacker. I haven't talked about it, Bill, but I'd like to now. Can we meet?'

Colin has a farm near Oxford, a clockwork farm, well run, nothing out of place and no hint of the violence he's experienced except, perhaps, the sign on the six-bar metal front gate –

WARNING. KEEP OUT. GUARD DOGS RUNNING LOOSE.
CALLERS STRICTLY BY APPOINTMENT.

Through the bars I could see a stone horse at the entrance, amid purple tulips and dead-headed stems. The cherry blossoms gave the place a sense of calm. It was quiet because Bertie and Quince, the two Alsatians, were caged.

'Those dogs are better than a gun when you're alone in the farmyard. They'll send a shiver up the spine. Quince is particularly vicious and vociferous. A sign of the times really. We used to have dogs that would lick you to death. Now we have a new breed.'

The farm is near a high-density housing estate for families with low incomes. Some years ago Colin, then 27, caught children damaging his property. After one break-in during school holidays, he kept a vigil at his barn the next day. He followed a boy on a bike from the farm to the estate. Colin wanted to question the parents. This twelve-year-old boy lived with his single mother and looked after his two younger brothers. The house was locked during the day because she had to work and all three children were forced to stay outside. Eventually they had decided to target Colin.

This wasn't Colin's first brush with vandals.

Another barn was burgled and ten thousand pounds-worth of antique furniture taken. The police did not inspect the scene of the crime and have not been in contact with Colin since he reported the theft.

Commercial premises on the farm were reduced to charred ruins in an arson attack. This time the police visited and were very sympathetic but told him to claim on his insurance and have made no report on their investigation.

Collin described a second, but failed, arson attack where vandals smashed a locked door, scattered paper around the building and set fire to a bundle of papers on an electric stove, but the fire fizzled out. Police responded by telephone only and told Colin he really ought to do more to protect his property.

Vandals have fired air rifles at his windows, set fire to hay ricks and slashed strings binding hay bales, which are compressed to keep out the elements. When the strings are cut the hay is ruined.

Colin's farm is bisected by the Oxford ring road, a section of which is a main route for the travelling community. He found a group with nine caravans starting to set up camp on one of his fields. They had used a bolt cropper to break padlocked chains on the fence. After the first three caravans entered the field he parked his Land Rover in the gateway to prevent others getting in. It turned into a chess game. They cut through another locked gate, moved on site and warned him: 'We're going to be here for six weeks. The first time you show your face around here will be your last.' After another incursion travellers threatened to kill his dog if he didn't stay away.

After four invasions by caravan drivers, arson, theft and a series of attacks by children, he feels under siege.

I started to wonder if we came from the same city. I live in the centre of Oxford; Colin was on the edge. But judging from the amount of violence he was describing, it seemed like we came from two different worlds. Yes, I had a death threat to deal with but that was the result of my investigations into the activity of a paedophile. I was the active agent who started moving around the pieces of that particular jigsaw puzzle. Colin was a passive victim, attacked because he lived in an isolated area and people thought they could get away with it.

Was this really what life was like for him now – an Oxford version of *Straw Dogs*, the Sam Peckinpah film where a young couple come to idyllic rural Devon and discover a cesspool of increasingly vicious local harassment?

Colin: 'Years ago people would come to the farmyard and lock their car doors, and my dad would say, "Where the hell do you think you are? You don't need to lock your car here!" Nowadays we lock everything – the barn door, the field gate, the milking shed and the petrol tank.'

He showed me the courtyard where a knife attack happened. His younger sister Annie, 25, was a keen equestrian and rose early to exercise her horse in the field where the family had built a miniature Hickstead, with various fixed obstacles for showjumping. A man in his thirties was trespassing. She rode up to him and asked what he was doing. He pulled a knife, a big one with a long serrated blade, grabbed the horse's bridle and forced Annie to fall. She broke her ankle, but managed to make the horse drag her five hundred yards to the farmyard.

On this bright clear autumn morning Colin was upstairs shaving. His parents were still in bed. Through the open window Colin heard the screams. 'I pretty well leapt from the top of the stairs to the bottom in one bound. I could see Annie hanging onto the horse pursued by this man, so I rushed into the yard and got between her and the steel blade to distract the intruder's attention and let her escape. I remember his words distinctly,' Colin told me. '"You're days are numbered. Do you want to be sliced with this?"' Colin walked backwards, away from Annie and the intruder followed him.

'There is a large chestnut tree near the house and my family had the habit of not putting garden tools away in the evening and just leaning them against the tree. I was abreast of the tree and a collection of forks, spades and shovels. I thought one of my options was to grab a garden fork or spade and thread him before he could thread me. You make all these instant judgements and assessments second by second. He saw my gaze going in the direction of the tree and shouted, "Pick up one of those things and you're a dead man."'

Oxford was starting to wake up on this autumn morn and so was Colin's sixty-year-old father who heard the commotion and immediately dialled 999.

'The intruder was watching me like a hawk. We were within three feet of each other, pretty much face to face. He was extremely riled and baying for my blood. I held this guy's gaze but in my peripheral vision I saw my father come out of the house behind the stranger, who was now level with the chestnut tree.

'I knew I could not even blink because this might give the game away that Dad was on the scene. Here was this man with a knife threatening me. If I made the wrong decision I might pay for it with my life and my father's life. Dad quietly sidled up to the chestnut tree, grabbed a shovel and went up behind the intruder who was shouting obscenities at me, and whacked him on the head.

'My poor father held this shovel with both hands so he pretty much lost his pyjamas, which ended up hanging round his ankles. I remember the ring of the metal when it hit the intruder's head. That was a solid shovel and the sound reverberated in this still space. I think even the birds had stopped singing; at least I couldn't hear them, only that hollow ringing.

'How he survived it I'll never know – adrenalin maybe. He dropped the knife and fell. Most men would have gone down and stayed down, but he scuttled sideways a few yards on all fours, to pull himself together, regroup and return for another attack. He had been hit very seriously and wouldn't be best pleased about that and I knew that even if he hadn't meant business the first time then certainly this time he did. That was the worst moment, when I feared it would end in something pretty horrible.

'In another moment I was facing the same situation all over again, and I knew I hadn't done very well the first time round. He was threatening to kill me and to kill us all, and there was no doubt of his intention and ability. If someone is coming at you with a knife and threatening murder, you look for superior power. It's a natural thing to do . . . so I asked my father to get me a gun. Our firearms hung in a rack on the kitchen wall, entirely legal and unlocked in those days.

'I felt the gun, a double-barrelled twelve bore, in my hands and aimed. It was an unpleasant experience, going against the grain. I wasn't used to encountering violence, to find I was propelled into violence within minutes and without time to think about what I was going to do next . . . I was not looking to escalate it or for it to end in a tragedy. Here are three or four minutes, they could define a life.

'I was brought up with guns, so I was very safety-conscious and knew never to point a gun at anyone, especially in anger. The gun was empty. I didn't have time to load it . . . even if I had wanted to.

'I stood there barefoot, wearing only jeans but no shirt, covered in shaving cream, with the gun pointed at the head of this intruder. He kept coming towards me shouting abuse – "I'm going to kill you. This is your last day." I could reach out and touch him, but instead I felt an urge to join in and give as good as I got.

'I thought I could be killed, no two ways about that. When you are facing a lunatic with a knife and there is no way you can communicate and all you have is a gun and a bluff, what do you do? I told him to get down on his knees and drop the knife. He refused. The stand-off continued.'

Colin described a scene that had the tension of a battle between a cobra and a mongoose. 'The police arrived within a minute or two but when someone is coming towards you with a knife it seems like an eternity.'

The stranger dropped the knife and went down on one knee. Colin was standing there, still aiming the firearm. The police didn't know what to think – who was the victim and who the attacker. Colin held up the gun and broke it open to show them it was empty, that they had nothing to fear and that he did not mean to kill the intruder.

'The police went over to the man and picked him up. They also picked me up. I knew I could be arrested and accused of doing wrong, because of the way I was brought up . . . but I had no choice. The cops immediately confiscated my two legally-held shotguns and kept them until two weeks later when the thug decided not to take action against me. They warned me that in future I would be brought before the courts if this happened again. The visitor was tried and bound over for five years in the sum of one hundred pounds after he admitted threatening to kill me. He was also ordered to stay away from our farm and our family for five years.'

There were so many knife-edge balances here, especially the moment when his father hit the intruder with a shovel, I wanted to know if he would do anything differently.

'Now that you remind me, I have to say it was a lucky day that could have all ended pretty badly. You do think about that but you shut it away. You don't want to talk about it.'

But now he was doing precisely that – opening it all up and on the airwaves – why?

'The Tony Martin story rang bells for me. I can see why someone who is vulnerable, living alone out in the country, having suffered these attacks . . . I can understand why someone would patrol their property with a gun at night, and I needed to get this small story out there in that larger debate, so it wouldn't be just my experience.'

Chapter 24

Russian Roulette

Foreign prostitutes in Oxford

Whore moans are on the rise in Oxford and brothels are creeping up amidst the dreaming spires of academia. 'Street girls' may walk around the Cowley Road, and gigolos may sip wine by an open fire in plush hotels in central Oxford, but the slightly safer end of the market – the oldest-established, permanent floating whorehouse – is opening branches throughout Oxford, including Summertown, where a considerable contingent of Nobel Prize winners lives as well as the current Metropolitan Police Commissioner.

This may be the safer end of the trade, but how safe? Oxford brothels do a brisk business-pay and display, as it were; so there is usually a stash of cash on the premises. Since this kind of business is unregulated and illegal, it doesn't have CCTV. There's the rub.

Two robbers targeted three local massage parlours where, according to the prosecuting barrister, 'sexual services were provided'. They dressed in balaclavas and carried a claw hammer, a knife and tubes stuck together to resemble a shotgun.

Over a three-day spree the pair got £380 from one brothel in Abbey Place and £500 from the Kitten Club in Headington. They met their match at a third house in Wolvercote, where one of the women attacked a robber, pulled off his balaclava and literally kicked him out of the premises even though he was holding a white plastic bag that appeared to contain a gun.

Brothels and brutes create shock-horror headlines and indicate the extent of the 'problem'. But turn the pages of the local press and you'll find adverts for 'adult services' that indicate the extent of the hypocrisy.

What do you do with a problem called Maria or Sasha or the Kitten Club, and why is it a 'problem'? Why should we consider a brothel in the neighbourhood to be a 'bad thing'? Some would argue if there were no brothels, the girls would be on the streets, and what would that do to the tone of the neighbourhood?

Others say that if sex workers are not being exploited, a brothel is a business just like any other. If a man decides he has enough money, £80 to £100, to purchase something that is not illegal and willingly offered for sale, what harm is involved?

After three years the penny dropped in North Oxford and people rang the programme to complain in an understated way about everything but the elephant called 'Sasha and Friends' in the corner of the bedroom – parking problems in narrow streets, pollution from people sitting in cars waiting in queues and noise, especially groans from first-floor open windows in summer. A few wanted to talk about human trafficking and women from Kosovo and Albania being forced into the sex trade.

Several locals were incensed and thought that a brothel was a magnet for morally bankrupt men and created a place where 'perverts are visiting until the early hours'. They went further and pointed out that 'this is ruining the reputation of our much-loved Summertown'; and they suggested a brothel would 'contaminate' the area, be a blight on house prices and a threat to the safety of their children.

Because a brothel amounts to opening a business 'on the wild side', the madams can get away with things that business people on the civilised side can't. They slip through all the loopholes: no insurance, no health and safety checks, no corporation tax, no VAT, no business rates and no planning approval. If anyone else but sex workers set up a business from home the Establishment would come down like a wolf on the fold.

Eventually fifteen police officers with truncheons drawn broke into the Summertown brothel and closed it down after confirming that no trafficking crimes were believed to have been committed. This did little to calm the natives; their cages had been rattled. But it did re-open a debate started in the *fin de siècle* by the Chief Constable of West Yorkshire police about legalising brothels. He argued that current laws on prostitution are absurd and that licensed brothels would get prostitution off the streets and allow for thorough health checks and taxation.

There were arguments on all sides. Back when the debate first started I wanted a second opinion from an expert, Cynthia Payne, alias Madam Cyn, who set up an infamous 'luncheon voucher scheme' for sex parties in Streatham.

'I went to prison for running those sex parties in 1980. The Establishment has been talking about legalising brothels ever since, but that's all . . . they never do anything about it. Now that someone with the status of Chief Constable has come on board, things might change.'

But why, I wondered, would someone inside 'the industry' – who was on to a nice little earner – want things to change?

'I do think it would be much healthier, and the girls could pay tax. Most of the girls I talk to are quite happy to pay tax provided they don't continually get raided and harassed. I've wanted it decriminalised for years, but because the AIDS business got so bad in 1984, I had to change my tune and say legalise brothels. I don't really want the state to run brothels because, let's face it, they can't run the country properly, let alone run a brothel. If they legalised it that means we could take anyone to court . . . the madam, the girls and the men.'

Since Madam Cyn had run several brothels, I asked her to explain what could go wrong to put people in the dock.

She was extremely matter-of-fact, not to say prim. 'I'm very good and experienced at running them and I wouldn't have girls that con men or roll them or steal money. I wasn't fortunate; I was just very careful. If that happened in a proper brothel, a legalised one, then of course the girl could be taken to court for it. Whereas at the moment there are a lot of things that go on in these clubs especially in Soho, where you pay about a £100 for a bottle of champagne and the man doesn't get anything for it. If that isn't fraud, what is?'

Madam Cyn had an overview of a particular underworld, and I wanted to understand how the clients might overstep the mark.

'If you give a man a fair deal and you do what you say you're going to do and give value for money, men don't cause any trouble. I can never understand when I get girls coming up to me and saying, "Oh, he punched me in the face or he did this and that . . ." I say – well, you must have done something to have got him in that state. They always deny it, but I've never had any trouble.

'I've discovered men were so grateful they'd found a decent place to come to, I never had that problem. And I had a good section of society, as you know; I had several MPs from the House, I had barristers, I had lawyers, and I had just ordinary working-class people, and I never ever had any trouble.'

In discussions with local government, business and charity leaders, one phrase keeps coming up like a bad penny – 'value for money'. But I wanted to know what exactly was value for money where sex is concerned.

'Well, if a girl says she's going to do this and that; and then when you go into the bedroom and she says she wants extra money to take her bra off . . . all this sort of thing, I mean, that must be infuriating to a man. No wonder some men lose their tempers and go for them.

'Here's another example. If a man leaves his wallet and someone in the flats steals it, most men will not go to court or to the police. We need to make men feel they can do that. If the Establishment tried to make brothels a little bit respectable, and prostitution will never be respectable, how many years have we tried? But if we made it a little healthier, perhaps all this fear and cheating can be eradicated. And of course if I were Minister for Brothels I would make sure that I allowed the police to come on the premises any time just to check that there's no under-aged girls.

'There are a lot of lonely people in the world, a lot of men who've lost their wives. There are a lot of disabled people, and I did have the odd occasion when disabled people came to one of my parties in wheelchairs. They weren't always thinking of sex; they just wanted to mix with people. That is the good side of it. It's not all sordid. It helps many people.'

I asked Madam Cyn if she agreed with the Chief Constable that licensed brothels would get prostitutes off the streets.

'There are thousands of millions of prostitutes. The older girls probably wouldn't like a brothel because on the street, in the shadows, they can hold their own in competition with the younger girls. In the dark men can't see how old they are. So I don't think they'll ever stop street prostitution.'

The Mothers' Union has strong views on this subject, so I invited Lynette Paul, their spokesperson, to put her case. 'We felt that if brothels were legalised it would create a two-tier system and Cynthia Payne has just agreed with that by saying you'd still have the older people on the street. Our major concern was that if brothels were legal, those who were sick or old would not be admitted and would therefore still be on the street where, of course, you would also have the under-aged.'

Madam Cyn could see no end to street prostitution. 'I don't think you'll ever stop it. Remember we're talking here only about legalised brothels, where girls could have an identity card to make sure that they have had the health check every month. If they were soliciting without that health card they could be sent to prison. At the moment they can go to prison just for being on the street.'

The fact that women could be jailed on the streets whereas men could go kerb-crawling wherever they wanted seemed slightly unfair to me.

Madam Cyn's voice rose to a slight peak of indignation here: 'You're never going to crack down on the men. Sex is too intense for the man, and that's what a lot of women don't really understand. It's very intense in men and it has continued to be. They can't shake it off, just like that. The government clamped down on the massage parlours in 1978-80 and that was a very healthy place for any man to go, a massage parlour, because you can't get AIDS through a massage. I mean the poor men; they've got to have something, haven't they!"

I asked Lynette Paul from the Mothers' Union if she knew why girls went into prostitution in the first place.

'We spoke to girls through the whole country and not many of them went "on the game" from choice. Many went because of poor family relationships; some were turned out of their homes. Most were unemployed and lacked education. We found a number of cases in many big cities where young couples with children had both been unemployed for years and were living on state benefits and unable to manage. The husband would mind the children while the wife went into the nearest large town to be a prostitute for one or two nights a week.

'The question we raised was how can they be better protected from violence and from the abuse of pimps. One of the suggestions that the Mothers' Union made to resolve this was to allow two girls to practise their trade from somewhere other than their home. At the moment that's illegal and the place would be classed as a brothel. One girl can sell herself to anyone she wants in her own home; that's quite legal. But we did wonder if that slight change of two girls from one house were made legal, it would solve the problem of pimps and violence.'

The problem of pimps kept coming up and they were clearly a big part in this equation. I asked Madam Cyn if she could tell me the difference between a pimp and a madam.

'Well, you've got a good point there. But at least a madam gives them a good home, well, not a home, but a safe place to work and she goes halves with the girls. At the moment she takes all the flack if anything goes wrong. She's the one that will go to prison and get the fines, whereas the prostitute will get off scot-free.'

Lynette Paul said most prostitutes didn't want to go on the game, but what was the view from a game player like Cynthia Payne?

'Initially, yes, they don't want to do it. But how many get out of it? You see, once a girl has gone into it, has gone over that line and she's done it, she'll rarely ever get out of it. But they do have their favourite clients and they enjoy the freedom that it gives them. Street prostitution, as I say I have come across it, and I think it is very sad; and it can't be too nice to be out there, especially in the cold weather.'

'It's worse than sad,' I said, 'I think it's dangerous in the days of AIDS.'

Madam Cyn had considered the danger aspect. 'And it's not just the street that can be dangerous, brothels as well. A girl got knifed in Mayfair and one chap who used to come to my sex parties picked her up and said, "Let me take you to a woman in Streatham where you'll feel a lot safer."

'This girl had been attacked twice. She was only twenty-one, a little Welsh girl, and she came to my house. After she found me I persuaded her to save her money. She got on her feet and I told her to save for a deposit on a house, which she has done. Now she's living in Wales quite comfortably. She's married and her husband knows nothing about this. A brothel is a place for them to go, but at the moment if a girl is desperate for money the first thing she's going to do is go on the street.'

When I mentioned the danger of prostitution, I was also thinking of AIDS and health checks or lack of them that could be dangerous for the whore and the client. Lynette Paul from the Mothers' Union: 'The medical checks will just give a false sense of security to the patrons because if you go to a legalised brothel you presume that there's going to be no sexually transmitted disease. But we all know you can test negative for HIV today and be positive tomorrow. So monthly checks are not going to be of any use at all.'

It was a hard argument to counter, but Madam Cyn reached for harm reduction: 'At least it's some kind of control. Currently anyone can run a brothel. Anyone can get a flat, put two girls in and an advert out and there's nothing to stop you. It might get raided after six months or a year, because you can't do nothing against the law without sooner or later being caught. But that brothel may run for twelve to eighteen months and there may be a diseased girl there or diseased man who's been there. That brothel could run for a year with no health checks and no control. There's nothing to stop anyone from running a brothel tomorrow.'

It's a dilemma that is one of those national 'no go' areas which combines moral choice, public health, sex trafficking, safety and harm reduction. The arguments are clear and passionate from all angles. The politicians don't make either an ethical or a practical choice, so the game of Russian roulette continues; and of course the result is that both prostitutes and clients die. That's the one thing that nobody disputes. So people take their case to the local BBC radio station and get it off their chests, but they never quite get it onto the political agenda.

Chapter 25

With my Paranoia Intact

How to ambush a radio presenter.

One of the essential traits for being a local radio broadcaster is a touch of paranoia to keep the guard up and sharpen the wits. Never let anything go through 'on the nod'. And of course some people are out to get you and they will usually be very polite about it. Even the most innocent invitation can be treacherous. Mostly the ambush happens on land, but I got caught in the air and underground.

Trouble can start in the most unexpected way. 'Hello, Bill, as our local BBC broadcaster in Oxford would you like to open a local village fête just up the road at the RAF base at Weston-on-the-Green? It will be a great family day out, so bring yours and they can watch you do some aerobatics.'

'What are aerobatics?'

'You get to go up in a glider and swan around the countryside, see the spires of Oxford from a different angle and get a new perspective on things. It will be magic.'

I agreed. On the day I ate lunch before the fete at 2.00 and the flight at 2.15; that was my second mistake.

The loudspeaker announced a spectacular show was about to start. I vaguely heard this and thought how sad I would miss it because I had just entered the cockpit of the glider and was sitting between the legs of Jamie, an experienced RAF pilot who told me we were 'going to have some fun'.

When we were safely up in the clouds, hovering above the crowd, Jamie asked me if I was ready. Not having any idea what he meant and not wanting to appear like the village idiot, I nodded; and then we began the spectacular show. First came the 'loop the loop'. We went straight up and up and up and so did my lunch. Then we went over, upside-down. I thought, Hang in there, Bill, just a few more seconds

It's amazing how easily we get lured into participating in our own downfall.

and it will all be over, or be all over, except it wasn't because instead of doing a complete loop, we did a 90% loop. When we were about to complete the circle and regain an even keel parallel to the ground, Jamie, nice Jamie, took us on a path perpendicular to the ground – what kamikaze pilots do when they dive bomb to their death.

We went straight down toward the crowd. I hate red tape and excessive regulations and health and safety officers, but the one time in my life when I needed them, where were they? We aimed straight for the cluster of what appeared to be ants from our great height. The last thing I remembered was a scene from one of my favourite films, *The Third Man*, when Orson Welles and Joseph Cotton are on top of a Ferris wheel in Vienna and the Orson Welles character, Harry Lime, says something like, 'Look down there. What do you see? A lot of small dots moving around. They look like ants. Now tell me truthfully, would you really care if one of those ants stopped moving forever?' Of course I always thought that was inexcusable, but what if one of the ants that was going to stop moving was me and not down there, but on the way down there? That might be worse than inexcusable.

At this point on the ground, one of those ants, my partner, was holding a bit too tightly onto the hand of our nine-year-old son on their 'great family day out' and thinking, This could be a spectacular death, and if there is a crash it will affect everyone here. It will be an horrendous, public way to die. How am I going to deal with my own private emotions let alone those of my son if he sees his father splattered right there in front of him?

The next thing I knew I was being helped out of the glider. Pope John Paul II used to kiss the ground when his plane arrived in a far country. After that experience I felt like I was in a far country and the first thing I did was to kiss my son when he ran up to hug me.

Another unlikely ambush came off the back of a curious challenge. 'Hello, Bill, do you agree the only reason to allow a person to have money and status is the wisdom with which he spends it? Well, since you have status as a BBC presenter, are you prepared to translate that into money and help a charity by doing a sponsored bike ride along the Nile between Luxor and Aswan and back?'

He had a point, and I agreed to be roped into this ride. However, the group bike ride of 500 kilometres which had moments of high drama, with armoured guards at the front and rear of the column, turned out to be much safer than my solo bike ride of just a couple of kilometres when we were back in Luxor.

I've biked and walked through some cultural and political minefields around the globe, but this time in Egypt I came across a sexual minefield underground, in a grave. I rode to the flood plain in front of the temple of Queen Hatshepsut with the hills leading to the Valley of the Kings behind me and the Nile in front. My guide book told me exactly where I should be, but I didn't realise what I was riding into.

The guardian of the tomb I wanted to explore was way ahead of me. He spotted me from afar picking my way around the rubble. He was probably weighing me up.

We descended through a hole in the ground, down some mud steps to a wire door that he unlocked. 'So, you're alone?' the guardian accused me. 'Where's your wife then?'

'She's sleeping.' Jane didn't feel able to cycle those five hundred kilometres in the Luxor-to-Aswan charity bike ride, so she stayed in Oxford. On Easter Saturday morning I thought she would still be in bed.

'I love friends,' he said, and was silent. 'Oh good,' I nodded, 'so do I'

– which took me nicely over some boundary or precipice that I didn't even notice I'd crossed.

In the absence of a switch, he joined a few wires to connect the Heath Robinson lighting system and we plunged into the tomb of Userhet, a royal scribe to the Pharaoh Amenhotep II. It was remote, isolated from the other Tombs of the Nobles in Luxor, and unexpectedly stunning, the carvings delicate and delightful.

In the main burial chamber hunters are caught on the wall in frescos, killing cows and ducks and catching fish. The chefs are cooking the feast and priests are pressing the wine. My guardian interpreted the ancient scene. 'These are grapes. They drink them. It makes the equipment big. They make love.'

I moved to a pillar with small carvings of bees in flight, but about to alight, with wings buzzing and feet poised to land for over three thousand years. 'Bees make honey,' my guardian intoned, 'and honey makes the equipment big.'

I stepped sideways into a corner where horses pranced on the walls, heads held proud, teeth barred, front hooves aloft and tails flying. The poetry in the movement was carefree and careful at the same time. 'They have big equipment,' said the guardian.

'And in here . . . this cave, the bedroom, they made love here.' It was a bit grotty. I had to duck down to my waist and enter the cave on my knees. He came in too and put his hand on my shoulder, 'Make love here.'

I crawled out quickly. In the underground labyrinth I mistakenly wandered away from the entrance. He followed. I was going up a blind alley, but at least I was going; motion held a kind of promise. That promise stopped when the lights stopped – Heath Robinson had let me down. There's nothing blacker than a tomb.

The guardian had the only torch. 'Come here. I want to show you something.'

I had a vague idea of the *objet d'art* in question. But where else could I go? I followed the light. It moved to a railing. 'Look,' he shone the torch down a hole.

I looked. He grabbed me. 'Careful, not too close. Twenty meters deep. Magazine for wine.'

I couldn't see the bottom of this hole before me. I was feeling dizzy and disturbed. I turned away from the cavern, but then of course there was no way forward and no way back. There was only my guardian standing in front of me with his torch piercing the dark.

'Don't be afraid. Come here.'

I couldn't. I couldn't move or speak. He came toward me with his light. I stood there in the depths of the earth, aware that someone was approaching me like an alien, his light probing, poking, prying . . .

Then suddenly, strangely, there was another light from another guardian with another tourist in tow in the distance. Obviously this Easter Saturday morning was going to be unexpectedly busy.

I made some noises and grunts and stumbled in the most promising direction. My guardian followed, 'I love you; don't you love me?'

'Actually – no,' I found my voice.

'I have small equipment,' he insisted.

'Oh . . .' I was clipped, if not clenched by this point. 'Exactly why are you telling me this?'

'Do you want to see it?'

'I've had a big breakfast and I'm feeling queasy.'

He didn't take the hint. 'I'll show you.'

'Why do you want to do that? Many people have small equipment. I'm sure you'll manage somehow.'

'Good,' he said as we reached the exit and those mud stairs again. He stood in front of me, blocked out the shaft of sunlight, raised his tunic, lowered his trousers and excavated his equipment.

Somebody had to lay it on the line for him. 'Well, considering the let-down you've given yourself so far, you're probably not doing half bad. Good luck.' With that I pushed past him, and flew off, like any culture vulture on slightly shaky ground, to my next tomb . . . with my paranoia intact.

Chapter 26

Optimistic Outsiders

Tony Benn on direct action and the Oxford ring road.

Direct action could mean 'I fought the law and the law won', but not often in Oxfordshire. When people decide to protest they get serious and grab the local airwaves. Over the last twenty years Oxfordshire people have been revolting regularly – against the Newbury by-pass, nuclear weapons at Greenham Common and the closure of community hospitals for starters. Injustice, inequality and idiocy by 'the Establishment' are often targets. But is BBC local radio part of 'the Establishment', a place where the voice of the local councillor will be heard across the patch? In short is it a 'safe pair of hands?'

Take the protest against Europe's noisiest road – the A34 – which runs across the spine of Oxfordshire and beside the village of Kidlington. This road had a brushed concrete surface with ridges so deep, it sounded like cars were driving over a rumble strip. The dual carriageway opened in September 1990 and from day one residents complained about the road noise being as loud as an express train operating 24/7. The government said 'we hear your pain' but little more.

L to R – the Oxford Professor of Scripture, me, Tony Benn and Billy Bragg leading a parade in Burford to commemorate more outsiders, the Levellers.

One listener put his head above the airwaves and argued the only way forward was direct action, a 'go slow' drive along this link road from the Southampton docks to the Birmingham markets at a speed of 20 miles per hour, side by side to block both lanes. Engineers, a retired policeman, school teachers, a local councillor, silver surfers, students and farmers in tractors rapidly swung into slow motion on the road. The protest set off every Wednesday at off-peak time for three months and ended up in *The Sunday Times*, on the desk of the Parliamentary Ombudsman and prime-time television news. As one local parish clerk put it – 'These are things that land on ministers' desks and give them grey hairs.'

After fifteen years of struggle, with a trail that wandered through BBC Radio Oxford studios to the European Parliament, the locals won. The government announced the re-surfacing of this section of the A34. But they won big time as well because their campaign led to the government stopping the construction of any more concrete roads throughout the country. The roar of the lorry on this road has been reduced to the pip-squeak of the Mini.

At the start of the debate I invited two people who could hardly be described as part of 'the Establishment' onto the airwaves, the then MP Tony Benn and Oxford environmental campaigner George Monbiot, nursing some recent wounds after the heavy hand of the law evicted him from direct action to create a people's park on the Guinness site in London. I wanted to know from the armchair theorist and the hands-on practitioner why people put themselves on the front line, what drives a person to take the risk to be counted in this way, and is direct action an effective tactic? I walked into this revolutionary minefield by asking Tony Benn why people are attracted to direct action.

'They do it because their interests are affected and they have no other way of doing it. If you go back into history, and you don't have to go far back, when people didn't have the vote, rioting was the only way you could draw attention to the injustices. Just look at the poll tax revolt in 1381, the English Revolution, the Tolpuddle martyrs, established trade unions, votes for women, when they were arrested, put in prison, went on hunger strike and were forcibly fed. More recently the poll tax last time was defeated because many people couldn't afford to pay it. If you look further afield at South Africa, it was all direct action.

'The thing is that people don't identify direct action with other forms of parliamentary action. You see, if a big business owns a plant in Oxford, they can close it tomorrow without a ballot or consulting anybody, and everybody's job is gone. Bankers gamble with the currency and that brings pressure on the government, so the term 'extra-parliamentary' covers a lot more than direct action by people; it covers direct action by the military, the media and by the bankers and the multinationals, and I think you have to put it in that context.'

Bill: 'You say it's been used throughout history, but there has always been a great cost involved each time.'

Benn: 'Well, I don't know about that. Our right to religious freedom was won . . . there was a man called the Reverend William Benn (I hope he was an ancestor) in Dorchester in 1662, and he wouldn't sign the Act of Uniformity. He was ejected from his living under the Five Mile Act and wasn't allowed to preach within five miles of a town . . . I mean all of our political liberties were won by defying unjust laws. In 1401 Parliament passed a law, the Heresy Act, under which if you were found reading the Bible you were burned at the stake. You see the trouble is we're not really taught our history. We're taught that all the marvellous things that have happened were given to us by kind kings and wise statesmen. Actually most of the progressive gains were made by struggle, and we're not told that. So when it comes up again at Newbury or the export of live animals or the A34 around Kidlington, which I know very well, people say "oh my goodness, what's going on?" It's been going on for centuries, but it isn't reported because it upsets the idea that the great and the good, if you are only kind and patient, will always give you want you want . . . and they don't.'

I asked him if he had ever taken part in direct action.

'Oh good heavens, yes! I mean all industrial action is direct action. I've spoken for the Liverpool Dockers two or three times. I did 299 meetings for the miners . . . they simply said if you're going to treat us like this, we're not going to work. I'll give you an example that is totally non-political to ease your conscience a bit. Take the ban on handguns. Now that was achieved by what happened at Dunblane and the public outcry. If there hadn't been a Dunblane massacre and possibly a Hungerford, although that didn't do it, we'd have still had handguns. But when something happens and peoples' minds change and they're really determined, the government and Parliament come into line.'

'Parliament, in my experience, is the last place to get the message. They never get it first because they're having a comfortable life and they're not affected by homelessness, poverty, destitution, injustice . . . so it's left to people to organise for themselves. I'm a great believer in non-violence, don't misunderstand me . . . I'm a Ghandian, but I still believe that non-violent direct action in an increasing number of cases is going to be necessary to draw attention to injustice to get it remedied.'

My response was that sometimes people involved in direct action shoot themselves in the foot because they go too far and lose public sympathy. Where would he draw the line during direct action demonstrations?

He was reflective. 'I think direct action demonstrations have always got a lot of "agents provocateurs" . . . you see the police dressed people up as printers at Wapping and they had masks, and threw bottles and then they disappeared into the fog; and that was the excuse for the police cavalry to come in. You can't be naïve about these things; there are some people who do cause trouble. At all the demonstrations I've ever attended people are told to be quiet, be sensible. But there is no doubt at Wapping. I was there I saw the police coming in with their flailing batons and shields and . . . well. . . it was a horrific experience.

'At Orgreave, you will remember, when the miners were accused of riot, the BBC put out a programme showing that three sets of bottles had been thrown before the police cavalry charged. During the trial at Orgreave, Arthur Scargill subpoenaed the police video with a time code and there had been three charges by the police before a single bottle was thrown. You see the media has a responsibility, and they do not report what they should do because they are part of the Establishment. You know, that's the awful truth of the matter. I hate to admit it.

'But I'm a great believer in non-violence and I would never countenance violence because I believe it would be wrong and also it would not be very helpful.'

I suggested he had pointed the finger at the Establishment and at the police, but not all people who are involved in direct action are whiter than white.

'Well, I don't say they are, but then neither is the government whiter than white. My God, the main terrorists in the world are governments. In 1956 Eden gave an instruction for the assassination of Nasser. I mean, this idea that if governments use force it's all right, but if anyone else throws a bottle they are in a different category! I'm not in favour of force. I am in my heart of hearts a non-violent person in every respect, but this idea that you can draw a distinction between the SAS going in and killing people and demonstrators who may throw a few bottles and then say the one is absolutely permissible and the other isn't . . . The only way you can get change peacefully is by having a democratic alternative, and increasingly democracy is being squeezed out of our life by a whole range of forces outside, which we are being told we have to accept, that's my feeling.

'There's a woman who was down at Dover, a Conservative, I think she's a councillor, certainly she was active in the Conservative party, and she turned up at the House of Commons, on the debate over export of live animals and said – "We were attacked by the police . . . now I know what happened to Arthur Scargill and the miners." You think that one out.

'When there is direct action the forces of the state are used to repress, and yesterday this eco-village at Wandsworth which George Monbiot is involved in, and which I visited two or three times, they sent the guys in with the riot shields to chase the demonstrators off because that field belongs to a rich company, Guinness, and these homeless people had no right to be there. You have to look at the real world. It would be lovely to think it was all so comfy and cosy, and governments do what they can and some people are a bit unreasonable . . . well, I'm afraid history isn't like that.'

Bill: 'Well, George Monbiot, your world isn't comfy and cosy, is it? You've just come back from direct action at the eco-village on the Guinness site in Wandsworth . . . what was it like down there?'

George: 'Yesterday was like a lot of evictions that I've been to . . . it was rough in places. I was tipped up on my head by the bailiffs and landed on a piece of wood, and I'm still feeling a bit fuzzy as a result of it. I think we left in a dignified and honourable way. We didn't offer any violence to the people who were taking us out and we managed to keep it rather good-humoured, which I think is a characteristic of a lot of the direct action movement. There's great humour, great creativity, and a great capacity for fun . . . and it often means that a situation which could turn nasty, doesn't get nasty at all as a result.'

Bill: 'Do you agree with Tony Benn that we'll see more not less direct action in the future?'

George: 'I think as people become increasingly frustrated with the government's incapacity to respond to people's very real needs in this country they'll see that the only option is to take things into their own hands. Politics is far too important to leave to the politicians. If we want to make change that really reflects people's needs rather than simply contributing to peoples' needs, then we must make that change ourselves.'

Almost on cue, Jim from Bicester rang the programme to say he was convicted of trying to free 'Rocky' from a dolphinarium in the north of the country. When newspapers took up the story and other supporters took up the fight against the dolphinaria and the public started to realise the cruelty of keeping a dolphin in a little concrete tank, these 'leisure facilities' started to lose money. Brighton, Morecambe, and Windsor Great Safari Park all got rid of their dolphins. Jim argued that as a result of direct action there are no more dolphins in captivity in this country.

I had another question for Tony Benn. 'We've seen in the Newbury by-pass direct action and now at Kidlington that a lot of people have green wellies and drive very expensive cars . . . seems like direct action is not restricted to a certain group of your usual suspects in society, but is something that is becoming more and more widely accepted.'

He agreed. 'I think that's true . . . and one case that we must mention is the Greenham Common women . . . very courageous women who camped outside the air base. They were arrested under the Justices of the Peace Act of 1361, for action likely to cause a breach of the peace. They were treated as witches and lesbians and horrible women. In Greenham Common there were enough nuclear weapons to destroy humanity. Now it turns out there were nuclear accidents at Greenham Common which have caused radiation to the local residents who didn't like the Greenham Common women, but those women were right.

'I think the educational aspect of direct action is so important . . . and there is one other factor, the media will no longer report public meetings and what demonstrators say but if something happens and there is trouble, then it is news with a capital N. I regret the fact that it has to be done, but frankly, with the situation we're in it's the only way of getting anyone to take the slightest notice of injustice.'

Then I asked if he thought there was a danger that direct action could be used by 'the Establishment' as a tool, a safety valve, a means of allowing people to let off steam?

Tony Benn was still optimistic. 'If you take an historical perspective most of these things end up as official policy ... I mean the environmental movement at Newbury has already led to a major cutback in the road-building programme. It's a pity people are not taught politics in terms of a totality, of what people do at the bottom as well as at the top, instead of just bowing and scraping to the House of Lords, the Monarchy and the members of Parliament. Actually life is about what we do here and now where we live, and not what somebody is going to do for us later if only we'll vote for them.'

George Monbiot's view was somewhat different. 'We make a mistake when we imagine that governments are here to give us liberty ... they are here to concentrate power, grab as much of it as they possibly can and keep hold of it as firmly as they possibly can. I think it is the job of an active and responsible citizenry to seize some of that power back and take back liberty from what would otherwise be a very authoritarian situation ... if we don't do this, we will get the most vicious dictators.'

Tony Benn didn't agree with George that governments only want power. 'The health service empowered people. Government took action and opened up access to good health care for everybody, free at the point of use. So I don't think governments are bad ... that's a very negative view. But governments do have to be reminded of people's needs and I think it's absolutely right to use direct action. These things are great fun ... not full of violent people. But, by God, the police repression is getting sharper and sharper and sharper. I just hope it doesn't lead to more repression because in that case we could be moving to a dictatorship of a different but modest and real kind that we have seen elsewhere.'

Thus ended the lesson on rebellion and the dearth of democracy brought to you by a slightly unsafe pair of hands from 'the Establishment'.

Chapter 27

In Thirty or Forty Years' Time
Victims of childhood sexual abuse.

Radio presenters tend to push the boundaries, kick over the traces. Exploring emotions and places that are off limits goes with the territory. If you spend your life on air going beyond the bounds, it's easy to do that in real life.

I've been with people where I've asked if any of them had ever been sexually abused as a child. I wasn't sure what kind of response to expect and what level of honesty, but I was surprised at how many admitted they had been assaulted. If my small samples are anything to go on, the scale of this problem is enormous. So, coming full circle, I brought it up on my radio programme.

Sexual abuse of children is an emotional minefield that triggers, every time, a sharp response about how we judge and punish offenders. But what of the victims? Who talks about the survivors and how we treat them? These young and vulnerable people have been hit and hurt. They know something is seriously askew because they're watching their lives fall apart and they don't know what to do. They are marginalised and don't have a voice, perhaps for many years.

When people have no place in a national debate, or have a grievance and watch punitive people hijack the discussion, where do they go? To local radio, because that's their forum for their problems. Nobody else is taking them seriously.

Carol rang to put her finger right on the central point: 'There is so little treatment available for people who were sexually abused as children. I was assaulted by my father many years ago, and I want to talk about punishing the abuser. You have discussed child sexual abuse before on your programme, and when the focus has been on the victim, there is very little reaction. When the emphasis is changed so that you talk about what to do with the abuser, everyone rings. This is something we need to look at.

'Treatment of abusers hits the headlines, but what happens to the victims, to those who have been abused, doesn't seem to have the same level of interest or emotion; and yet the abuse goes on and on with us, year after year. It never leaves us.

'One woman said she would give the abuser to the families to punish. It is actually a fact that there are more cases of child sexual abuse by members of families than there are by strangers. Abuse takes place mostly within the family, so to whom is she going to give the abuser for punishment because the families often collude?

'One of the problems we have with abuse is that it is hidden within families in our society. It's not an open subject. We will talk openly about punishing abusers, but this idea of abuse within the family is not talked about openly, and I feel really strongly about that. If you have a moment I'd like to read some poetry I've written about the faces of abuse. These are parts of longer poems I've written, which will perhaps give people some idea of what it is like to live as an abuse survivor.

'The first one is called A Fractured Face:

> *Fractured face lives fractured life.*
> *Fractured eye sees fractured world.*
> *Fractured heart broken in two.*
> *Fractured eyes cry fractured tears.*

'The second excerpt is from another poem called *Child's Face*:

> *Child's face, shining tears showing hurts from the start of*
> *   time.*
> *Child's face, trust betrayed by those who gave her life.*
> *Child's face, my face, from so long ago, still there inside:*
> *Hurt, betrayed, unloved, abused,*
> *Worthless, fit only to be used . . .*

'And that's what it is like to be a survivor of abuse.'

I said that I found it very difficult to comment on her poetry and I just wanted to think about it for a while. Carol was not ready to accept that and asked me why I found it difficult to say anything. I told her the poetry was pretty raw stuff.

Carol agreed that it was raw: 'But shouldn't we be commenting about it? Isn't that what the problem is with abuse – that it is raw and so we hide it away?'

I could tell from the way she talked about abuse being hidden away, being a secret, that she wanted to scatter the cobwebs and discuss it in public; so I asked her if she got help quickly when she was abused or did it take years.

'I didn't get help. I told only my mother and she didn't want to believe me. She gave me a good hiding and said if I ever mentioned that again I would be sent away. So I locked it away inside myself for many years, deliberately . . . because there was no other way I could deal with it. What else could I do as a very young child but forget about it? Eventually it came out as a very severe depression. I was fortunate to have a GP who recognised the problems and found a therapist for me. But that therapist was not available on the NHS. I've had to pay privately because the NHS does not provide intensive one-to-one therapy on a very long-term basis for people suffering from a really bad depression from long-ago causes.

'I had to pay for it, and my financial circumstances have changed after I became ill through the depression – I lost my job. This was after I started the therapy; but the therapist made it clear that if I couldn't pay, if I had a hard month, he'd waive the fees. Now I call that commitment on behalf of the doctor, but the treatment is not available on the NHS.

'I'm nowhere near the end of the treatment. It's taken me four and a half years of three one-hour sessions each week. There are pitfalls in therapy. It's hard, really hard – like having basic major surgery. It has to hurt before it heals; and the trouble is that the surgery goes on for a very long time if it's done properly.'

The question that nobody could ask is what actually happened . . . it would be too intrusive and too graphic. But I did want to understand something about the abuse and the means to exorcise it. Was time a factor? I asked Carol how long this abuse went on.

'We don't really know. It was for a long time and probably started when I was about three; and it probably went on for several years. The total facts won't come to light. I don't even now have a very good recall of what's happened, although I do remember quite a lot of it. The mind is a funny thing. It can shut things away in compartments so you can forget it and get on with your life.

'Actually bringing it back is a very stressful thing, but it's a thing that you have to go through; and you've got to have somebody there by your side, which is where the therapy comes in – somebody who is very reliable. I still have some very bad days . . . I was and am very depressed, really quite ill. An enormous amount of anger is locked up there, of course. They say depression is frozen anger, and I think that is quite a good description of it.'

I wasn't certain which of her parents would be the focus for that anger. Her father abused her, but her mother refused to help her, so I asked what kind of relationship she had with her mother.

Carol didn't hesitate: 'I don't have a relationship with my mother. Not a real relationship. It's all surface. I didn't speak about my abuse for forty years. I remained silent in case her threat came true and I would be sent away. I think most mothers do know what is going on in child sex abuse cases, at least subconsciously.'

I suggested that kind of complicity, that ability to allow the abuse to continue, or at least not to stop it, could be as bad as or maybe even worse than the actions of the abuser.

Carol: 'Maybe, and as a society we all know that it's going on and we turn a blind eye. That is what I'm trying to say: we need to turn around and face this. It's like what I said about your programme – when victims are on, people don't react. When you discuss the punishment of the abuser there are lots of phone calls and that makes a statement to me. We are a society that is interested in punishing the offender and not in empathising and helping the victims. We profess to be, but we're not.'

Carol was lucky in a way because she was getting help; she was turning around and facing her demons. But not every victim of child sexual abuse receives the kind of help that they need.

Greg rang the programme and his voice over the airwaves was bristling with anger: 'I'm forty-five and I had an experience when I was six that absolutely wrecked my life. I was raped by a man and I was never able to talk to anybody about it at that time. Since then I've never been able to form a relationship with any male figure both at work or at home, and it's left me isolated from male society.

'I've had every kind of therapy including hypnotherapy on several occasions and it really hasn't had any effect. I still live with the horror of that experience even to this day. In my case therapy actually made the rape worse because it brought it home vividly over and over again to the extent that every time you talk on air about sex or about gays . . . everything like that hurts.

'The therapists took me back to that period, that moment in time of the rape. It was extremely painful. They took me back over and over again on several occasions, but it did not relieve the horror. It meant that from that moment on it was just more vivid in my daily conscious life . . . and it still is to this day. I can't get away from it . . . it's affected my whole life. My father died a couple of weeks ago and right up to the moment he died, I was unable to tell him about this. It was something so horrific because it separated me from my father.'

A lot of problems were intertwined here, so I asked Greg if he were able to get rid of the anger, would that help him deal with his relationships.

'I don't think so. I've got a very strong faith and that has helped me be able to forgive the person concerned; but there are psychological associations. The man who raped me had bright ginger hair and was Irish. I have an absolute aversion to people with ginger hair now. My father had ginger hair. It gives you psychological connections that are very hard to remove.

'I have to deal with a lot more than anger. Every time I see someone with ginger hair or an Irish accent it will depress me and push my stress buttons. For a long time, about twenty years, I wasn't aware of what was happening to me.'

If he knew about this upset and anxiety, but didn't know where it was coming from, I wondered if there was a moment when he turned around and consciously confronted the fact that he had been raped.

'Until this one day when I was twenty-six I never told anyone about it. I was married and for some reason I decided to tell my then wife. I broke down and the experience made me face it. She was horror struck and couldn't believe it but said it did account for a lot of the things in me that she couldn't explain, like the fact that I had no male friends for a start.

'I still don't have any male friends. I still panic if I'm left alone in a room with a man. I can't sit in a car alone with a man. Even with my maturity at the ripe old age of forty-five I know I am not threatened by any of them physically. I'm strong enough to deal with any of them, but

I still feel that anger and anxiety. I still feel a cold sweat coming out.

'Here's an illogical thing . . . I've even tried to provoke an outlet for my anger. I know a gay bar in my town and I've been in there fully aware that I'm hoping one of them will make an advance on me so I can really mess into him. It's that bad. It's so pent up in me . . . and it's only my faith that helps me to control it and exercise a kind of forgiveness and offers some peace of mind.'

Greg had mentioned his faith several times as a framework to understand what happened to him and to move on, but he was going round in circles. I wanted to know more about his faith, which was Christian, and centred around a male figure of God. How did he deal with that?

'God the Father denotes a caring presence, a father in terms of someone who is looking after us. Jesus Christ was a man because the male figure was the dominant one in society at that time. I don't think it is significant that Christ was a male; and his life is so obviously one of loving that it's not a threat to me. However I don't know how I would feel if the figure of Christ were present in my life in real material, physical terms as a man. I've got Christian friends, men, who from time to time in loving gesture have given me a hug, and I've felt myself cringe inside even though they were Christian people I knew.'

I asked Greg if he had any children, and he said he had been married three times and had a child by the first marriage, a boy. 'I have no relationship at all with him. I see him maybe twice a year at most and when we meet we can hardly talk. Everyone I've told about this has tried to help but without success. After all this time I realise that I've just got to live with it.'

He didn't sound like someone who was coming to terms with the childhood rape, the words unspoken to his dead father or the love he can't give to his son. His voice had the sound of the rage of someone who's 'just got to live with it'.

Greg: 'People talk about children being sexually attacked. They talk abut the trauma there at the time and the trauma for the parents. But we never talk about the on-going trauma to the child. Never. We don't discuss how it's going to affect their life for the rest of their life.

'No matter what happens after the moment of that rape, nothing removes the scar from the child's mind. Nobody can anticipate how it's going to affect that child because we're here only when it happens, and we don't look into that child's life in thirty or forty years' time.'

This subject of child sex abuse tapped into a deep reservoir of experience among many people who rang to tell their story about their scars. Not all of these scars involved abuse. Judy rang to say she had been assaulted, well, not actually assaulted but threatened, by a naked man.

'I was walking with my baby sister in a garden at my college, Magdalen, and we were trapped. There was a very high bank on one side and the river Cherwell on the other. We were standing on a path between these two when a man came out from behind a tree, a very big, naked man, and started running towards us.'

I knew that area well because I used to walk there. It is isolated, very beautiful in an eerie way. There was a locked gate at the end of this path and a fence.

Judy was incensed. 'I must say my overwhelming emotion was rage. I felt instinctively he would go for my sister who was much younger than me and much more vulnerable. I was just so angry. If he lays a finger on my sister I'm going to slay him.'

'We reached the gate before he reached us. Since I'm a member of Magdalen College I had a key and I got it open in two shakes, only just in time. I slammed it shut, but he tried to get through afterwards. If we hadn't got out there would have been hell to pay.'

There is one house in the area, an old mill house. Judy and her young sister rushed to the house opposite and hammered on the door. The woman wouldn't let them in for some time. There is a large deer park that extends beyond the path and her house and it's a lonely place. Judy told me the woman had children and was frightened for their safety. 'I could see they were well protected with a high wall around her garden, but she wouldn't let me in straightaway because she had been disturbed by strange men leaping over the wall and exposing themselves.

'Eventually she let us in and we reported it to the police. They had a very unhelpful attitude. The policeman asked me how I felt and I was quite straightforward and told them I felt furious and so angry. I felt rage possessing me at the thought of this naked man forcing himself on my little sister.

'The police couldn't accept that and kept saying things like, "Well, you know he's more to be pitied than you are in that situation." And they wrote out this statement that was full of things like "I was very frightened" or "I just wanted to get away as soon as possible" or "I was not really in complete control" . . . that sort of thing. And, my goodness, I was in control. I got that gate unlocked in two shakes and I went straight over and banged on this woman's door.

'I'm not sure which was the worse experience, the naked man chasing us or the policeman helping us.'

These and several other stories all focused on the unresolved anger of the victim and the disturbance that this left in their lives. But why would people talk about such private matters in a public place? Mostly this subject is a big secret, and they all wanted to break this taboo and stop the silence that surrounds child sex abuse. They raised the curtain on a dark area that most people don't ever see, but the darkest area of all which they highlighted was the lack of help – counselling and therapy. It seems that when someone grabs a child and pushes them over into the abyss of abuse, there is no safety net, no long-term strategy and nowhere to talk about it.

Chapter 28

Dreams and Nightmares
Brian Aldiss, Stanley Kubrick and me.

Local radio presenters are a bit like Rosencrantz or Guildenstern, minor characters who wander around the action, moving a scene on and providing links, useful foils, but not really players, more facilitators, even celebrators.

Oxford author, poet and screenwriter Brian Aldiss celebrated his 70th birthday by bringing out his 70th book. So I invited him to discuss his career on air and asked him why he wanted to be a writer in the first place.

'After ten years of public schools, five years in the army, most of them in the Far East, you are unfit for normal society. There's nothing much you can do, but become a science fiction writer.'

He was his usual feisty self so I suggested that in a sense his writing does have an element of arrogance in it because he wanted to change the world, didn't he?

'Oh yes . . . yes . . . absolutely so. Well, I'm a very humble chap but I'm also a very arrogant chap. We're all rather divided personalities, don't you think? We're not robots or androids. We're very complex people. Thank God. Rejoice in it.'

Brian is complex all right and about the same age as Dennis the Menace. Dennis is static, poor little chap, stuck in childhood for ever; but if he had been allowed to age he might be akin to Brian who looks innocent enough but we know he's guilty, an avuncular figure awaiting the return of the mini-skirt, a person whose eyes tell you he's always played with fire.

I decided to ignite a little spark. 'One of the complex parts is what goes on when we're asleep. . .the dreams. I gather your philosophy can be summed up in "I dream therefore I become". What do you mean by that?'

'Well, you have to take note of your dreams,' he began. 'Sometimes they're quite trivial, reflecting as it were the events of the previous day.

But every now and then the symbolism is very profound. Now what is this symbolism? It's the actual unit of currency that exists between the phylogenetically ancient parts of the brain, the old parts of the brain which knew no language, and the upper parts of the brain, the neo-cortex, which exists only in mankind.

'Those two parts of the brain have a certain amount of difficulty in communicating with each other. This is why, for instance, when you become really angry, you do things that perhaps you don't mean to do because the neo-cortex, the intellect, is switched off and the old instincts of the old brain take over. The way a dog will fight, you will fight.

'So the essential of sleep is that we will dream and these symbols are traded between the old part of the brain and the new, and you are well advised to take account of what you dream because in many cases the dreams are the truth about yourself, often unpleasant, as are many of the things that we suppress in the day and come out in dreams.

'That is where your true self fights with the persona, the mask – no I don't want to use that word – the persona that we use in daylight hours. So pay attention to your dreams. They are where you will find the truth about yourself.'

Some people have just a hint of science fiction in the way they lead their lives. I suggested to him, 'You seem to be, I won't say at ease or comfortable with the old part of the brain, but you seem to have a certain fascination with it.'

'Oh certainly so. Yes, the more one studies, the more one becomes aware that underneath the self that you've become since birth, let's do away with the DNA bit that you inherit, the physical things . . . you also inherit a psyche that has been formed over thousands of generations of experience. Now people know this. People actually know it intellectually. We talk, for instance, about the seven ages of man: the youth, the teenager, one of the notorious ages of mankind, onto your slippered dotard, aged seventy onwards. These are all roles we fulfil in life, whether male or female. They actually govern a whole part of our personality.

'We like to think of ourselves as kind of intact, one person acting in society, but we are so much embedded not only in society, but also in all that has happened to us in the past. Does that make sense to you? You're looking a bit . . .'

I was preparing a new question. 'No, I'm not ... I'm wondering how my next question fits because out of that struggle we come to something you said earlier. We're many people and we're contradictory people. How would you describe the contradiction that is Brian Aldiss?'

'Ah ... well ... I don't know.' He paused, waiting to catch that particular ball and bounce it back. 'I mean I have said in the past that I was struck by a line of Pushkin's ... he said he wanted to lay waste the hearts of men – that's what I really wanted to do, but I discovered in myself the fatal art of entertainment, and this is the two sides of me, you know: the clown that wants to play Hamlet, but equally Hamlet who wants to play the clown.'

I knew these two sides. Some years ago, in another life, I ran a small chain of art cinemas, one in Oxford was called the Penultimate Picture Palace, and I invited Brian to select a series of science fiction films to correspond with an annual outpouring of artistic talent in Oxford called Artweek. We produced a programme stating that 'Brian Aldiss, best-selling science fiction novelist, will introduce the programme and reveal the season's surprise film around midnight'.

The surprise film was *A Clockwork Orange* by Stanley Kubrick. This was in 1988 when Kubrick was still angered by headlines quoting judges up and down the country who said that muggings and rapes were on the increase due to copycat violence based on actions by a gang on screen called the Droogs.

In 1974, just three years after it first hit the cinema screens, Kubrick withdrew his film from distribution in Britain, and it was still banned in 1988. Brian managed to get around that by obtaining a video print through his American literary agent. I hired a projector that would blow up the print to a reasonable size for a cinema presentation and we would get around any legal restrictions by showing the film for free.

Our small attempt to unfurl the flag of artistic freedom and allow people access to banned art stirred deep passions. This is how *The Sunday Times* columnist and critic Joan Bakewell saw it:

Oxford's Penultimate Picture Palace is risking Kubrick's severe disapproval in showing it, free, each midnight in its current festival of sci-fi films, as part of Oxfordshire Artweek '88. The programme is rich and serious: Tarkovsky's *Solaris*, Scott's *Alien*, as well as Kubrick's own *2001: A Space Odyssey* and *Dr. Strangelove*. The context is one of serious cinema-going. And the Picture Palace is a film club. The fear of gangs of marauding youths taking their cue from the film to don bowler hats and go on a vicious spree is unfounded. But Kubrick still won't be pleased.

In fact 'explosive' is the best way to describe the reaction of Stanley Kubrick working through his film distributor Warner Brothers. I received an injunction forbidding me to show the film before the first screening.

Brian Aldiss described that moment. 'You and I were standing out in the street waiting for the punters to come along, which they did, in droves. Then a limousine pulled up and two men in pin-striped suits got out; they were Stanley's hard men. You hadn't even shown the film yet. I can't think you had infringed any right and if you were going to, you hadn't at that point, and still they slapped this writ on you.'

Within a matter of days a court summons arrived with an invitation to appear at the Chancery Division of the High Court. It was more like the High Circus. The court case was adjourned so that my solicitor and I could meet with Kubrick's 'representatives' to sort out a 'deal'.

We were invited to a tasteful office building near the Courts of Justice where people might well arrive wearing bowler hats. After ritual formalities we were escorted to – the basement. I wouldn't say it was a modern-day torture chamber, but your screams could not be heard through those thick walls and there was heavy security. We reclined on leather sofas under low domed ceilings of what must have once been a coal cellar. Cucumber and salmon sandwiches appeared on silver trays and we exchanged pleasantries.

It was a very English event. I can't tell you precisely what happened for legal reasons, but I would rather encounter that gang of vicious thugs, the Droogs, from *A Clockwork Orange*, than meet these 'representatives' again with or without sandwiches.

I agreed not to go into court and fight the case and Mr Kubrick, with the subtlety of a sledgehammer, got his way. I did not then show *A Clockwork Orange*, which is now available freely on TV, video, DVD and at the cinema.

A few days later my solicitor and I found ourselves in need of a literal sledgehammer. Stanley Kubrick wanted us physically to destroy the video and produce the evidence of destruction. So I took the tape along to my solicitor's oak-panelled office in the heart of Oxford, opened a brown bag and put the tape of *A Clockwork Orange* gently on his desk. Then we looked at each other – how would we destroy the video in a way that would satisfy Stanley Kubrick?

We both thought of a fire in his wastebasket, but there was the small problem of smoke detectors. So we hit upon the idea of a hammer, but in this sedate suite of offices in central Oxford no one had one handy. We tried jumping up and down on the video, but this plastic was tougher than our shoe leather. Finally some helpful soul located a sledgehammer and we took turns ritually slaughtering this copy of *A Clockwork Orange*.

How did Brian Aldiss react to it all? The person who described the film as 'perhaps the most powerful science fiction film that people in England are not allowed to see – normally' and who procured this copy of the film that was now lying in tatters said the whole thing was ridiculous.

Brian had worked with Kubrick in the past and I wanted to sift through their relationship for some clue to the way this particular drama was playing out, so I asked Brian how he came to work with Kubrick.

'Like most things in life it was sort of accidental. He was interested in a short story of mine called *Supertoys Last all Summer Long* – only 2000 words but it's got this great title, and when you think about it, what actually happens when winter comes? Well, winter came to me in the shape of Stanley Kubrick.

'He invited me to lunch in the mid-eighties. It was interesting to see Stanley then. He was dressed very much like Che Guevara with massive, curly hair and a beret on top, in fatigues or a camouflage outfit. He said, "I want a thumping big bestseller of a film about which I can still maintain my reputation in society", meaning the sort of respectability he'd gained by his own banning of *A Clockwork Orange*. He wanted *Supertoys*. I really didn't want to sell it to him because I felt this was just a cameo and he couldn't make a blockbuster film of it.

'Stanley argued that he had done this with a short story of Arthur C. Clarke's called *The Sentinel*, which eventually had become *2001: A*

Space Odyssey. I didn't think he could do that with *Supertoys* because it is an inward story. Clarke was looking out to the galaxy. I was looking inward to what it's like to be a child.

'Anyhow in the end we did the deal, a very difficult and secret one . . . I couldn't consult with my literary agent, I couldn't consult my lawyer. Something was drawn up and roughly speaking it was that I would make two million pounds unless someone else contributed a few lines to the film. Then I'd get nothing. It was quite clear that this was a win-win situation for Stanley. However by this time I was curious, so I signed everything and went to work with him. I wanted to work with a genius to see what it was like.

'After about ten months of working together daily and after many scenarios, he told me it wasn't working and said, "I'm sorry. This is it", meaning I was fired. He lit another cigarette and turned his back on me. He couldn't even say goodbye. I can't tell you what I actually think of Stanley, but I do know he was obsessed, he was so anally oriented if that's the word, very, very tight-fisted, and there was no way you could reason with him. Once he'd made up his mind, that was it.'

So how did that assessment – secretive, obsessive, tight-fisted and a man with whom Brian could never argue or discuss anything – square with my own experience of Stanley Kubrick? It was certainly one side of him that I recognised, doubtless there were many others. But of all these virtues, or vices, obsession is the one that stands out.

Brian agreed: 'Why was it that Stanley was so obsessed with my little short story *Supertoys Last All Summer Long*? It preoccupied him for ten years. Why was that? I wrote this for the Christmas number of Harper's Bazaar in 1968 and I didn't think of it again until two decades later he comes up with it. Why that story? I can only think it's the story of a little artificial boy whose mother doesn't love him. It's the kernel of that story. Now was that what preoccupied Kubrick? Once I started to analyse it I thought, yes that's my story, actually. I had a mother who – whatever I did – really couldn't love me.

'I don't know. I'm only guessing . . . but ten years he spent on that; and then despite his boast he could make it into a film, he died; and Steven Spielberg turned it into *A.I.: Artificial Intelligence.* That poor small child at the heart of it is a sort of ghost, isn't he?'

Chapter 29

The Paws of a Dilemma
Are big cats roaming the Oxfordshire countryside?

Was I a lightning rod for every crackpot in town, those single-issue people magnetically drawn towards the airwaves? I certainly felt like that when people started calling to report sightings: 'I was on this lonely road in Otmoor during broad daylight' or 'I was sailing on the Farmoor reservoir when I spotted . . .' or 'I was washing the dishes and looking out the window . . .'. The tone was always one of quiet determination and certainty. Who were these people and why did they want to testify, as it were, in public?

Some subjects conjure up a depth of passion and deal with immediate problems like vivisection of animals and fox hunting. Others touch on fundamental feelings and generate a sense of fury or religious fervour, like abortion and gay marriage. I can understand why people bang on about the MMR vaccination because it affects their children. And when callers wax lyrical about the benefits of cannabis and call for the drug to be legalised, the pleasure principle could be at play. There is always a reason that propels people into the limelight and makes them take a stand in public debates.

But big cats? Which callers are going to put their heads above the parapet and talk passionately about why they believe pumas, cheetahs,

Do big cats live in Oxfordshire?

leopards or panthers are roaming the countryside? There's nothing in it for them.

James walked into my programme off the street to agree. He was a sceptic. 'I've always relegated big cats to the same sort of league as UFOs, ghosts and Lancaster bombers on the moon. I've been very cynical about it. Until last night . . .

'I was cycling home from work between Witney and my village in West Oxfordshire, and have done most days for the last four years.

'At 6.30 on a November night it was dark. As usual I crossed the little bridge that spans the disused railway line near Curbridge. As I drew parallel with a gap in the hedge on the right of the road, I heard a noise that was – without exaggeration – one of the most frightening things I've ever heard, a low-pitched, hissing, spitting noise.'

James didn't look like the type of man who's easily frightened – six-feet tall, well-built and fit, close-cropped hair flecked with grey, with plenty of confidence, a man who could easily be at home in a pin-striped suit or motorcycle leathers.

'One normally gets an idea of the size of something from the sound it makes, and whatever this thing was, it spat and hissed and sounded large, deeply angry and very threatening. I looked at the area where the sound was coming from and I could see in the gap of the hedge a large, hunched black shape . . . I would guess the size of an Alsatian, but indistinct because it was dark.

'I was petrified. I yelled at whatever it was as loudly as I could and kept yelling. When I got home I was quite hoarse and barely able to speak. I put my head down, gripped the handlebars and with an explosion of adrenalin I must have gone from fifteen to thirty-five mph in two turns of the pedals.' It was a reaction that could have put James in great danger, but I would discover that only later.

He was still disturbed and recovering from shock, and I wanted to explore how he dealt with it.

'I got home shaking like a leaf. That scared me absolutely witless. I'm now reluctant to cycle that road again. I will do, but I've just gone out and bought a very large 'D' lock, a heavy shackle lock. If I need to belt any animal with it, that animal would stay fairly well belted . . . and I've bought a very loud air horn as well, just on the off-chance.

'This is probably utterly irrational and stupid; but however I analyse it, I can't get away from the fact that I felt too much like prey for my sense of comfort.

'I don't believe in ghosts or the supernatural, but big cats are not something you believe in. These animals are either out there or not. I do know that I was terrified by what I saw and heard. There was no growling, no roaring, just a hiss and a spit, the sort of noise you get from a leopard in a jungle film . . . that kind of sound and magnitude.'

I suggested that the sound had gone straight into his brain and lodged there.

'Yes, right into the subconscious. The sound was absolutely primal and triggered every kind of primeval element in me. That was cave man – sabre-tooth tiger – I'm out of here. It was at that sort of level. I spend my day being very rational and balanced as a company director of a consulting and marketing firm. My reaction was neither rational nor balanced.'

'What do you think it was?' I asked.

'Of course, it could have been a trick of the wind. I could have imagined the shape, although not the noise. Feral cat? Maybe, but if it was, it was seriously big. Badger? I don't think badgers hiss. Definitely not a dog. I felt like prey. For God's sake, this is West Oxfordshire. Are there panthers roaming wild in the Cotswolds? I don't know. I really don't know . . . but if it was, and from everything I've read they are one of the most efficient killing machines, then I'm very lucky to be alive.'

James put me in a difficult position. He felt able to walk into my programme and say that because I'd known him for years, there was a mutual bond. He was a friend and I had a lot of respect for his powers of analysis and understanding and here he was shaken to the core. Something had happened, but was it all in the mind? Could his imagination have conjured up a big cat?

The discussion moved from sound to sightings, a few miles away at a medieval manor house. Juliet, the lady of the manor, said that when she saw her first big cat 'it was so unexpected that I would have been afraid, but I was overcome with curiosity. I was taking my little terrier for a walk around the lake in our garden mid-afternoon on a sunny afternoon in late spring. It was sitting across the lake, twenty-five yards away on a mound covered with those little yellow flowers that come out in spring, anemones and buttercups.

'After a while this big black cat with a low-slung body, an extraordinary long tail and little pricked-up ears, rose, slunk to the top of the mound and disappeared down the other side. We found a paw print and made a cast of it, but unfortunately that broke.'

Juliet is sixty-eight and organises the house and garden of their 192-acre estate from her office in one of the farm buildings. About a year later she caught sight of a big cat while working. 'It just came down the garden path from the greenhouse. It must have been winter, there were no leaves on the trees. I got a good long look.

'The animal knew its way around and went straight to a tarmac area that caught the sun's rays and sat down.'

Juliet described herself as 'not given to overstatement'. She was chair of the Parish Council and chair of a weekly day-care centre in the village, but she said her grown-up children 'still scoff at me for the story'.

She spoke precisely and vividly, in a way friends have described their dreams to me. It was so matter-of-fact, so well framed – 'walking down the garden path', 'knowing its way', 'finding a hot spot to sun itself in mid-winter'.

Of course Juliet has unimpeachable credentials and I wanted to go down that road with her, but was it the Cotswold version of the Yellow Brick Road, tasteful honey-coloured slabs leading to a parallel place that doesn't quite exist? That was my question, not my judgement. The jury was still out because Juliet didn't strike me as a dreamer.

So far there was no corroborative evidence. Each experience involved one person. Sally shattered that barrier. The Glyme River runs alongside the North Oxfordshire town of Chipping Norton where Sally lived, near her three grandchildren. 'We can walk out of our house right down the Glyme Valley. I was with Felix, my eight-year-old grandson, and we entered a nature reserve which was all very wild and you had to push your way through nettles and things.

'We came to a clearing and suddenly saw this black creature going across the open space in front of us. It was as least as big as a fox and the spectacular thing was that it moved with its tail straight out behind.

'It was loping along quite slowly and its tail was as long as its body. It didn't pay us any attention, although I was wearing a red anorak, some mucky trousers and gum boots, and probably stood out a bit.

Felix saw it as well, and we couldn't quite believe it and said, 'look,

look, look'. Then it went off into the undergrowth. It was early summer and there were quite a few leaves on the trees, so we couldn't see through the undergrowth. But we did have a good view. It was early afternoon in broad daylight, not particularly sunny, but good visibility. We saw it for about thirty seconds to a minute.

'Felix and I talked about it and agreed we were not seeing things, that it really had happened. We got quite excited and went back home and looked it up in the encyclopaedia. We think it is a puma.

'I've always wanted my grandchildren to take an interest in nature and now Felix is dead keen.'

There was a lingering doubt that travelled the spine of this story. Sally is a pillar of the community in Chipping Norton and did a great deal to help with the flower festival at the medieval church of St. Mary's during the millennium and she's done work with the Citizens Advice Bureau; but was she a bit eager to see something?

I know she came from a family in colonial administration in India and her father was a Ghurkha. Maybe Sally inherited her practical and precise approach from her father. She was certainly methodical and so was her description of the 'puma', but was it a projection of her desire to make her grandchildren 'dead keen'?

Probably not, I concluded. She was too self-possessed, up front and honest. Something had certainly happened. But what exactly?

The story shifted quickly from a grandmother to a groundsman. 'I've heard different stories and rubbish spoken, but what I saw was no mammal from this country and I know 'em all,' was the way Stephen from Moreton-in-Marsh opened his case. 'It had just gone dark about eight o'clock in the evening, and I had gone past Sarsden, heading toward Chipping Norton. On the left-hand side where the old estate wall is, I saw this pair of eyes looking at me. I ground the vehicle to a halt, and I saw this animal staring. It had a box head and small ears on the top with big green eyes, and I mean large green eyes.'

I challenged him on that; he was very emphatic, too much so perhaps.

'If you've ever seen an animal in the dark you remember the eyes. I'm lucky enough, some might call me unlucky, but I've worked with dogs all my life and I've hunted about every animal in this country. These eyes were nothing like any other mammal's eyes. They were like a bush baby's eyes, large green reflective eyes. And I saw this animal which was the size of a medium wolf, a large Labrador. It was fawn in colour with black points. It had a bow in its back and pump-handle tail. The animal stared at me and I stared back at it in complete astonishment.'

I was curious to know just how close this encounter had been. Stephen told me it was twenty feet. But even if he had been that close, since it was dark how could he tell about the box head and the ears on top?

'It was in the lights of my van, which were on full beam. This animal was right in the middle of the road. There's a turn as you come up a hill from Sarsden House with its long estate wall and trees. As I came round the corner I caught it in my beam. That was forty feet away. Then I slowly came to a halt which was about twenty feet away. It looked at me and then turned and moved like a cat moves, not a dog, deer, fox or badger, and went through a gap where those old gates are at the estate.

'I sat there for a few minutes and then I got out of my car. I took my hunting dogs – two Glen of Imaal terriers – out from the back and they went ballistic. They were on the scent of something and were going crackers, but I wouldn't let them go because the cat had done no harm. It really was just to see if I had been dreaming.

'I went home and kept it to myself. A few days later I was going to Chippy and decided to stop at the police station because that big cat could have got out from the Cotswold Wildlife Park, for all I know. I spoke to the wildlife officer who was eager to see me; he asked me to keep our conversation private, but I wasn't disbelieved.'

I tried to get Stephen to tell me the angle that the policeman was taking on his story, but he was adamant and at the same time his tone took on a note of quiet success.

'The only other sighting was while driving from Shipston-on-Stour back to Chipping Norton about quarter to six in the morning. I came up to the bridge where the old Chippy railway was and I saw this big black creature cross the road and then take a straight four-foot leap over the old railway wall and disappear. I followed it with a beam, but I could only hear some crackling as it went off. The old railway lines are a good habitat for big cats, all covered with growth and not much gets down there except a few walkers.

'I was walking down the old railway at Bourton-on-the-Water with the dogs and I was looking up at a lowish tree about fifteen to twenty feet high and couldn't believe my eyes. There was a muntjac deer lying across a branch ten feet up. You tell me any mammal in this country which can carry its prey up a tree. I don't know any. That deer was dead and just hanging up there evenly balanced in a 'U' shape. You tell me how a muntjac gets his back end torn out and gets up a tree.

The weather-beaten face was becoming more animated and his hand movements short and sharp, chopping the air in agitation.

'I started off on the farm. My father was a herdsman, and as a young lad I assisted him and then became a herdsman with cattle and pigs. I'm a hunting and shooting man, and I've worked with the hunt as a keeper and terrier man . . . been working with animals all my life. I know how they move, and when I watch an animal move I can tell you what kind of animal it is. This was a big cat. A cat moves with consummate ease, virtually a prance with silent foot falls. They do straight leaps, like the cat that leapt over the four foot high wall. No dog could have done that from a standing start.

'I was sceptical about big cats for a long time. I'm not one of those ufo-logists; I'm a very practical person and I look for the practical answer.'

He claimed to be one of the biggest sceptics in the past; I wondered how he would describe his position now.

'I've had to think hard about discussing this because I've seen people tell their stories and I've heard people snigger at them and say big cats don't exist. Well, I've seen 'em. I've seen two – the first one for about twelve seconds, the other for about eight, and I know what I saw – two total flukes, to be honest – and I'm not asking anyone to believe me.

'I can't explain it, but I feel honoured to have seen them in a way. It was fantastic to see what I saw. It took me three or four days even to admit it to myself. I wasn't looking for a big cat. I've never looked for one in me life – I'm not interested in that, and I don't go looking for them now. I was very lucky.'

These and several more big cat sightings prompted one Oxford man, Steve Archibald, to set up the Oxfordshire Big Cats Research Project. He told me of a recent sighting at Ditchley Park, a rambling country estate of fifty-five acres near Oxford, used by Churchill during the Blitz. Much of the parkland is overgrown with long grass, mounds and ponds and it has a bit of a magical wilderness atmosphere.

'This lady was walking her dog, a saluki. This Persian greyhound would normally be on a leash because its hunting instincts are so strong, its prey drive so fierce, it will even chase deer. The smallest movement of a rabbit will trigger it off. But on that day it was off leash. She walked around the corner on one of the risings at Ditchley Park and the dog was right by her, cowering between her legs and didn't want to go anywhere.

'When she looked up there was this big brown cat right in front of her, about twenty yards away. She just stood there and didn't know what to do – stay or go. This is quite common with people who have a face-to-face meeting with a big cat.'

He was hitting a point that almost everyone who rang me brought up, so I asked him what, exactly, should people do.

'Just retreat very slowly, because if you have eye contact with it and you're going towards it, you are threatening it. So you need to be passive, keep your eyes down, open your jacket up and make yourself look a bit bigger. Don't turn your back, and don't bend down because that shows the back of your neck. If you are stooping that could trigger an attack response.

'In North America, especially on Vancouver Island, some pumas have attacked people on mountain bikes in the hills. They are crouching down and moving along at speed. The bikers look like they are on all fours and showing their backs and the nape of the neck. Your earlier guest, James, who heard a hiss from a hedge while he was on his bike at night, would have had the same sort of silhouette as a gazelle, especially when he was cycling at speed. He could have made himself into a prime target.'

I mentioned that foxes are now coming into towns and cities. I've seen them in the roads going up to rubbish bins to collect the odd meal and I could see the population of foxes swelling. If big cats are out there in the countryside could they ever stalk the streets of Oxford?

Steve said that a couple had already reported a sighting in the Summertown area of North Oxford, near the Dragon School. The couple were retired professionals, who wouldn't be out of place in an Alan Bennett piece. He dressed in yellow cords and brogues with a cardigan, shirt and tie. She was a medical doctor, usually dressed in blue trouser suits and practical shoes. The woman was the first to eyeball the cat.

'Their garden backed onto a field that went down to the River Cherwell, and on several nights when they relaxed in their conservatory with a gin and tonic they could hear this amazing screaming. She described it as a cross between a woman screaming and a baby crying and a rook. It was resonating all around the area. Well, that's the classic description of a mating call of a puma.

'She's got two black labs and the last thing one night she let them out for a wee in the garden. When she opened the door the dogs shot out. Then while she was standing there she could hear this screaming again. The dogs came bowling back inside and stood shaking in the basket. So she went into the garden for a look and saw something under the yew tree. She stood there looking and didn't know what it was, so eventually went back to the kitchen and kept an eye out through the window. Something came out from the yew tree, walked across the lawn. The security light came on and it was a big black cat that wandered over to the dry stone wall and jumped over.

'The next night they were having another ritual gin and tonic in the conservatory and this amazing screaming started again. So the man went out into the garden and saw the cat sitting on the wall. I don't know how many gin and tonics he'd had by then, but he went running at it and said, "Shoo, go on, bugger off" and after that he told me, "We've never seen it again".'

This cast of characters helped turn my radio programme into a verbal safari for a time. As stories of many more sightings continued to roll in, I was faced with a dilemma. Either there is a small population of various kinds of big cats – panthers, puma, leopards – living, hunting and mating in the Oxfordshire countryside or all these people who report sightings are cranks from cuckoo land or deranged and deluded.

After talking to the callers and visiting some of them I got no sense that they wanted to convert anyone or whip up support for their views. They weren't normally public people. They knew they were taking the risk of being ridiculed, and yet they had experienced something so strongly they simply felt compelled to open up.

Maybe they were the 'lucky ones', being in the right place at the right time for a few moments to catch sight of something seriously strange.

I don't know what happened to these people. But I do know what happened to me: I don't feel like a lightning rod for every crackpot in town anymore.

Chapter 30

Love and Death

Falling in love over the airwaves

Love is a tricky area, especially when people go there on air. I don't believe in love at first sight, but what about love at first sound? When you come across that voice which is so sensual, assertive, rounded and rhythmic that you feel more alive whenever you hear it, what happens? Is it possible to fall in love on the radio? I ask because that happened to me . . . maybe.

My twenty years on air mean that I've been broadcasting for about 17,000 hours. There are probably people in Oxfordshire who have listened to me more than they have listened to their husbands or wives.

One person who tuned in for almost all of those twenty years didn't have a husband, but she did have opinions about each subject that came up. I met her on the airwaves during my first week, when she seemed to emerge from a cloud of sparks, hurling her words like Jupiter his thunderbolts. She argued with the force of a barrister hellbent, or laughed like an angel about everything – raising children, Hiroshima and Nagasaki, Margaret Thatcher, hanging, the Pope, prisoners of war, blindness and music. The more we talked, the greater the space we created on air where we could meet as equals and enjoy each other's company.

When she cared about something, she was passionate, and she cared about the programme I presented. When the local BBC managing editor wanted to change it, she decided to tell him to keep his hands off. When she arrived at the station, I bumped into her at the door accidentally. There was Margaret, dressed all in blue and smelling of lavender, so naturally I gave her a big hug; and that was it. That was how she signed all her letters afterwards. Even when she went totally blind and someone else wrote them for her she always added in her own hand the sign for the big hug.

Years later when her relatives asked me to speak at her funeral, I told them that was the moment we began our 'chaste affair'. She was in her eighties, I in my forties, and we began a journey that we both knew would end sooner rather than later in death. We fought every step of the way about everything, often about death itself.

I don't know how she died, but if she did fulfil her wish for voluntary euthanasia in her ninety-sixth year, then I am content. Margaret changed my view of that by looking at principle through pragmatic detail in one of her last tapes to me

Hello Bill,

I still listen to you although I no longer attempt to ring in. I should be unlikely to be coherent. I wanted to talk to you personally today, but if you are too busy, chuck this tape away. It's not important.

Recently I unearthed a whole pile of our recordings dating back twelve years or more. I found them fascinating, the huge variety of subjects is indicative of the kind of programme we had in those days.

There are, of course, several on the subject of death from various angles, which particularly interested me, and of course we disagree fundamentally at almost every point, and I wonder very much how you would feel about the situation I am in at present. Since Christmas, my first born, and very precious, niece – more of a daughter than a niece – has been slowly dying of an extremely rare form of cancer – peritoneal – and she is unable to eat or drink anything at all. She is now just bones with a thin covering of skin, with a lot of pain, particularly now in spite of the doctors' splendid efforts to give her every comfort that they can.

I can't speak too highly of the care that she is having in this quite wonderful hospice, with nurses at her side within seconds of being called and three doctors all looking after her. I think that is the reason she is still alive.

I won't distress you with the details of the ghastly

additions of discomfort and problems which are arising now. Of course, if she were a dog the RSPCA would have prosecuted us long ago for allowing her, and the doctors for allowing her, to go on suffering the way she is.

Listening to your discussions on tape with me, you seem to think there is some value in prolonging the life of a person, however unhappy and in whatever discomfort, for the sake of their relatives who may want to hang on to them. Let me assure you that Diana's relations, particularly her three brothers, are the last people to want to keep her alive. We are all praying for her death. And of course, as far as I am concerned, we had sixty-four happy years of her companionship and her health. During the last five or six years since my own disabilities have increased so much she has been so protective about me and has done so much for me constantly, looking after my various wants and coming over here whenever she possibly could.

And the sad thing is that I cannot persuade her to allow me to go and see her now . . . she's dead against it because she's convinced it would be too difficult for me to make the journey and cope with that. I see how she feels, because I'm very much more frail than I was and so blind and so deaf and getting around and communicating with people at all is a great problem. However, of course, I want to be with her and holding her hand if that's the least I can do. But she cannot be persuaded to allow that, and so I feel totally isolated here.

Her husband, who's a saint, rings me up everyday and gives me a detailed account of how she is, but I can't even communicate with her. We've tried on the telephone, which is impossible because of my deafness, and I have sent her one tape, but there are problems about playing it in the ward. And so I am out on a limb really unable to do anything for her, although of course that's the one thing I want to be able to do.

And yet you suggest on your tapes that there is some value in prolonging the life of a dying person for the sake of her relatives. This is a total puzzle to me, and I do wonder if you were ever up against a similar situation, which heaven forbid, you might feel differently.

You may or may not remember that her sister, who died of lung cancer when she was thirty-eight, leaving four young children, was able to arrange for her death, very peacefully in her own home with the collaboration of her understanding doctor, and that of course made all the difference to the family. If only somebody could do that for Diana. She is sixty-four now, but that is no age, and she has no children, which is probably a good thing.

I do hope that there are enough people in this world who do not take your view to enable the law to be changed, but it would not be in my lifetime. Anyhow, dear Bill, I don't know why I am bothering you with this, but listening to our discussions and our total difference of outlook I can't resist telling you what the situation is for me now.

Needless to say, this doesn't require any acknowledgement, but I do send you a lot of love. You've been such a prop and stay for all these years and still are . . . so a big hug, as ever,

Margaret

Chapter 31

Shorty

Richard Attenborough opens up a closed area: himself.

John Lennon said 90% of life is 'just turning up on time'. For a broadcaster the question is whether or not my august visitor would turn up on time and if he did what would I call him. I've had problems in this area. The former local MP for the Witney constituency, now Lord Hurd, came in for a talk about his book on Sir Robert Peel and told me beforehand he wanted to be known on air as 'Douglas'. I bottled it and kept calling him 'Lord Hurd' until finally he said over the airwaves, 'Do you know, Bill, that my name is Douglas?' It was more of a command than a question.

So when I interviewed Lord Attenborough I asked at the very beginning, 'How shall I address you?'

Without a moment's hesitation he shot back, 'Shorty, or even Baldy

Lord Attenborough, with me and Chris Gray, Arts Editor of the Oxford Times, *after 'Shorty' and I had both recovered from our interview.*

... but certainly Shorty.' How was I going to deal with this one? Here was an icon of the cinema, Oscar-winner Richard Attenborough, suggesting we go for the unexpected. That opened a trap door in my mind and I wondered how far to push it.

I was offered an interview when he came to inaugurate a new arts centre in Oxford, The North Wall, at St Edward's School in Summertown. I thought this would be a short sound bite. Thirty minutes later everybody there was almost in tears. His words wove a spell over the small group listening and nobody moved, perhaps for fear of breaking something. He told a story about himself, but it chimed with each one of us. We all knew those moments of childhood that are magnetised and shape us into who we become, but mostly we keep them hidden. We don't want the pain.

He began by connecting education and art. 'Education means getting out to people and making them aware of something that exists in creative terms not viewer terms. Arts as a touchstone, as a way in which we can find out what the other person thinks and what he cares about ... that I think is terrific and any form of expression of art which allows us to state our credo, our beliefs, our prejudices, our antagonisms, that can put them out there and have the debate in an art context, I think that's really worth it.'

I was sceptical. I wanted to know where politics fitted into the jigsaw – could you have a political debate in the arts world?

Shorty: 'Oh dear, that is such a difficult question. One of my gods is Chaplin, and the difficulty is that in my world of movies, film is not a fine art. It's a semi-art. It's an art form of the current century ... We do have, as Chaplin saw, an ability to reach numbers of people in relation to what we think, what we believe, and what we are doing, as nothing else has ever done ...

'So if we accept that fact then you say . . . OK, we are in an entertainment medium . . . without entertainment we don't have anything. Why should people come and sit in a theatre like this – beautiful as it is – if they are not challenged, if they are not captivated by what is being presented. But if it is an art form – and if it is to be a major entertainment communication throughout the world – then it has an opportunity, in answer to your question, to be able to make the plea for compassion, to beg of toleration.'

Clearly he had a whole world hidden behind those words because they came out so powerfully.

'If we don't use those facilities to say what we care about and what we believe in then we are denying the genius of the invention. I believe there is always the possibility of being able to enlighten people who have never thought of something before, as Chaplin did, so that suddenly this wonderful genius, actor, comedian is making *The Great Dictator* or even *City Lights* . . . anything that he touches and does makes a comment on the human condition . . . If the cinema doesn't do that then it should give up and go away.'

Of course, he refused to give up or go away. I knew some of the details of the struggle to bring *Gandhi* to cinematic life and I asked him what he achieved with that film.

Shorty: 'Gosh . . . I don't know. It took people by surprise. It took twenty years to raise the funds and get the script that was required for such a project . . . I remember going to a dreadful head of an American studio and I can't use the language on the BBC. After I told him what I thought about the subject and why it was important and worthwhile making it, he paused a moment and said, "Well, Dick, we've done a lodda things together and we audda be able to help you, I'm quite sure. But Jesus, Dick, who the hell is interested in a little brown man dressed in a white sheet carrying a bean pole?" Well, that was a fair way of summarizing the attitude of the industry.

'I think *Gandhi* worked because . . . he brought out into the open this question of non-violence; but also he believed the truth was actually the only vital thing – whether you arrived at non-violence, which he thought was inevitable if you examined truth – then your life and your attitudes and the success of the human race had a chance. What the film did was to introduce this to a vast number of people. He focused the debate on moral issues, of politics, of humanity, of self respect, of the dignity that each human being is entitled to in terms of food and water and clean air.'

Bill: 'You've looked at this man, Gandhi, and you've had a canvas and you've painted a picture of his life. Let's paint a picture of yours.'

Shorty: 'Oh my God . . .'

Bill: 'What colours would we use?'

Shorty: 'I wouldn't do that . . . it's an unpleasant vision . . . let's talk about somebody else.'

I could see a man who was uncomfortable but I wasn't going to give up. Then again, I couldn't force him to answer if he didn't want to, and I didn't have many weapons in this battle of wits. I did, however, have the power of silence. I sat there with my microphone running, looked into his eyes and simply kept quiet.

Shorty: 'What do you want? Ask your question again.' The first question started in a strong voice; the second ended fairly faintly, on something of a dying fall.

He was struggling – not with me or with the question, but with something else. We were coming to a cliff where one of us would have to take a leap over it or one of us would have to back down. Still, I didn't say anything.

Shorty: 'I don't quite know what you're after.'

He rolled his eyes to the ceiling and when I met them again, I could see a tinge of terror. Perhaps most people who interviewed him simply didn't go that far. I continued to sit in silence.

Shorty: 'I can't talk about me!'

Bill: 'Why not?'

Shorty: 'Oh, because it's a boring subject . . . no, no, no. I can't talk about me. We can talk about things I've done, been involved in, but not about me.'

Bill: 'That's interesting. . . because what you do in your films, particularly with *Gandhi* is you strip away layers to get to the core, and that's what I'm trying to do now.'

We looked at each other for a while, and it could have gone either way. He sat back in the chair, looked over to George Fenton, who wrote the music for *Gandhi* and was the inspiration for this arts centre he was inaugurating, and cried, 'Help, George.'

And then he began. 'I'm very conventional. I'm a traditionalist. I adored and hero-worshipped my parents. They were liberal with a small 'l'. My mother was, to a certain extent, a suffragette. My father was a very early member of the Labour party, and I joined the Labour party when I came out of the air force in 1945; and I'm a passionate supporter of the principles of Labour.

'But it goes beyond that in this way . . . my father was principle of a University College, he was at The Other Place in Downing College. He was a choral scholar, he believed and Mama believed that they were privileged people. They weren't well off. I think the Governor's salary was £1,500 a year. They believed that the inequality of revenues and therefore of facilities, and therefore of opportunities, was unacceptable and whenever you were able to demonstrate that you could share that with other people then it was worthwhile.

'So we never went on holiday, my brother John, my brother Dave and I, without a boy or two boys from somewhere in the city of Leicester (where we were) who had never seen the sea. We always went with somebody.'

The words were coming fast now, like a torrent. He was in a place where I suspect the sights and smells and sounds of childhood were as precise and vivid now as they were sixty or seventy years ago.

'I remember my mother was horrified by the Spanish Civil War and used to march down the main street in Leicester under the hammer and sickle, protesting against Franco. She brought sixty Basque refugee children to Leicester and set them up in a great hall, and raised funds to take care of them after the bombing of Guernica.

'My father loved German literature and music. He adored it and used to go to Germany and became aware in the late twenties and early thirties of what was happening in Germany and started to bring Jewish refugees to England and formed a committee and had Jewish people on the staff of the University.

'Dave and Johnny and I had just come home from school and war had been declared literally a day or so beforehand; and we were told to go to the Governor's study. Well, that usually meant I was going to get a thick ear for something I had done or hadn't done at school. Instead of which he said, "You boys, you know we have these two girls in the house who are on their way to their uncle in New York. The war has been declared, there are no more passages to America. So we have to decide what to do with these girls. Your mother and I think that what we should do is to adopt them, not legally, you know they call us Aunt and Uncle or whatever, not Mother or Father because we hope their parents will come out of Germany (but of course, they never did) ... and so boys what do you think? It does mean a number of things. It means we can't go on holiday for quite so long as we usually do because instead of being a family of five we are a family of seven. Shoes will have to last longer; clothes will have to be patched up. There will be sacrifices and there will be jealousies and you will find that this is very difficult . . ."'

I didn't ask if it was difficult because a certain softening of his face told me that yes, it was, but it was worth it.

'My mother said, "Darlings, we adore you, as you know, we are a very united family but there will be problems. You will be jealous because you know how much we adore you, but we have to give love to Irene and Helga, the girls, to a much greater extent than we can even give it to you because they have nothing. You have us, you have the love and the security and the knowledge of our love. They have nothing. They can't go to America; they certainly can't go back to Germany. And so are you prepared?" Here my brother David and I looked quickly at each other. The girls were quite good-looking, and the decision was immediately yes! We unequivocally would love these two girls to come and live with us, and they did. Irene and Helga became our sisters and lived as part of the family for eight years.

'I don't know why I've got into all this, but you asked me a question about what I care about and I care about the manner in which my mother and father conducted their lives and I have attempted . . . failing inadequately . . . but I have attempted in my life and my work and in what I do to try and demonstrate how aware I am of how fortunate I am and my desperate desire to try and share some of that, and equal it out a little.'

Maybe he didn't know why he got into this space but he was no longer resisting it. I knew by the way he sounded; there was a slight smile behind the voice as well as serious sadness. I felt there was some way to go yet.

'I went to Mozambique on what's called a goodwill visit . . . it's a ridiculous title, I know, but I was a Goodwill Ambassador for UNICEF. And I remember walking down a passageway between hovels where people were living under a piece of canvas or under a piece of corrugated iron with sewage running down in the pathway between the two . . . And I asked a dreadful, awful, banal question that one's ashamed of immediately because there you are in shoes and trousers, and fed, and I was about to talk to a huge black woman who was hammering out Coca Cola tins and, as I say, idiot that I was . . . but I was embarrassed by virtue of my circumstances . . . she so self-evidently had nothing . . . She was going to give these tins to a little child who would run up the hill and obviously hope to sell them . . . and I said – oh, I am so ashamed to be mentioning it to you now – "Is there anything . . . if you had a wish what would you wish for?" At least I thought she would say clean water or some food or work or clothes . . . and almost without hesitation she said, "Education for my children."

'I thought, I am so embarrassed, I am so ashamed of how little I have ever contributed to other people's welfare, and trying to be in some way of help and assistance. I often wonder . . . we're in St Edwards School, we're in Oxford, we're in the UK . . . do we actually know how fortunate we are, are we actually conscious of how important education is to that woman who had absolutely nothing? And she had the perception and the feeling and the intelligence to know how vital education was.'

I kept his eye during all this, but I wanted to look away. I wanted an interval. Here we were in this beautiful theatre space of The North Wall with rows of empty seats. It would soon be open to the public. Perhaps quietly with these 'noises off' we were laying down a challenge or raising the dramatic bar for other stories that would occupy this space.

'Why I'm telling you this story, I haven't the remotest idea. I don't remember what you asked me . . . It was something to do with Gandhi, and then I said, well, it had to do with my parents which is true. Most of my life I suppose I'm quietly ashamed of the fact that in some measure I'm motivated by wanting to justify myself to my parents and to say – "Darlings, I am aware of who you were and what you did and what you stood for and what you contributed, and I am a disappointment in that I was anything but an intellectual." Academia was a foreign world to me except he was eventually Vice-Chancellor of Leicester University. He would have loved me to go to university, passionately believing in the value of education in its broadest sense.

'The arts were a huge part of our lives. My mother was president of the local drama society. Father had wonderful conductors, Beecham and Sargent and people, used to come to the University and talk and my mother played the piano and would accompany Mary Jarrod or whoever it was on piano, and the arts and the education were as one at home.

'So in a way because I left school at sixteen or seventeen and went to RADA and went to the Air Force ... Dave and John, bless them, were the academics and they fulfilled much of what the Governor stood for and cared about ... I didn't. I was a clown at school. All I wanted to do was to perform and ultimately I think there must have been a feeling of "Oh dear, what a pity Dick didn't have a job to do, didn't do something of some value." So perhaps when I do do *Gandhi*, or *Cry Freedom*, or *Lovely War* or *Shadowlands*, they are about things that he would have liked me to examine.

'My apologies for the length. Jesus!'

I thought, *his* apologies? That's nice! What do I do? I can't apologise now, but maybe I should. He'd allowed me into a private place. Maybe I had overstepped a mark and pushed it too far. People can feel exposed, maybe even betrayed in those circumstances. Perhaps I should apologise to him ... but I kept my silence.

Chapter 32

Expectations

How well do you know your employer?

When Auntie Beeb took me in hand as an infant broadcaster twenty years ago, we started on a journey examining everything along the way, from the humour of Barbara and David Huelin and their cheap and cheerful funerals to the death threats against me. Everything was fair game. 'Don't hold back, Bill, but be fair.' The only thing I didn't examine carefully was my own relationship with the BBC. I was too busy going out, pouncing on people and ideas. I didn't stay in and find out what expectations we had of each other.

Do we ever really get the answer to that kind of question? Mostly not, but I happened to be one of the fortunate few, if that's the right phrase, to stumble across something akin to the heart of the matter. And what did I do? Well, it was so terrible, I just carried on as though nothing had happened.

If you ever want to cross over from the world of the workers to the realm of management, you need to act when the membrane between the two is thin, stretched to its maximum, when they are changing the guard. You also need a guide with a sense of humour, who knows the system and the loopholes. Mine had the name of a tree, but I called her 'Willow' because she could bend and scrape and sway in opposite directions on command.

At the BBC the alpha animals are always roaming around the top of the jungle, playing musical grape vines. In my twenty years at BBC Oxford there have been four different people in charge. With each change of leader comes a pattern of other changes. Colour stands out; we've gone from white walls to off-white, to yellow and now to red. The furniture invariably changes, from metal to wood and back to metal. Then the content changes; filing cabinets are cleared out, desks are turned upside-down. It is possible to hoard a bit of information from one regime to another, but eventually you are found out and it all has to go.

Willow was called in to throw out all offending files after the third changing of the guard. She made mincemeat of the production office and reduced some staff to tears, but she didn't stop there. Willow marched into management territory and demanded the surrender of all the old staff files. This was a rich vein. There were tons of stuff on some staff. My own set of files ran to four. The skip was getting pretty full by this time, so Willow called me in and handed me all my files with the suggestion that I put them in my toilet area for 'appropriate reading or use'. The folders were full of news clippings and headlines about Heine which I recognised, and a few knife-in-the-back letters from a Lord Mayor of Oxford calling for my dismissal and labelling me inexcusable, dangerous and insufferable.

One managing editor had a white file and a black file system for certain employees. The black file was there for him to dish the dirt if any were needed. I had a black file, two even, and among some unusually nasty stuff I found a photocopy of what appeared to be page 233 of a book, I couldn't find out which book, but a name, presumably that of the author was almost legible at the top of the page, something like Mills or Myles. That was it; a page from some unidentifiable source. The three paragraphs on this page focused on the relationship between Jack Kerouac and Allen Ginsberg and discussed the 'beat generation' in New York, including their sleeping, financial and drug problems involving a certain Bill Heine.

The last paragraph was highlighted with a box drawn around some sentences, but the first part set the scene.

> Allen [Ginsberg] and [his lover] Peter were to leave New York on March 23, 1961, and Peter managed to kick his heroin habit just in time. Allen made complex arrangements for Lafcadio, Huncke and Janine. He paid the rent on the apartment until the end of March . . . but without Allen there to take charge, everything fell apart the moment he left. Huncke and Janine were both injecting Methedrine into the vein, and Allen's money

> simply disappeared . . . Janine and Huncke got themselves
> a place with Elise in a renovated tenement building.

The next part of the paragraph was highlighted.

> Bill Heine moved in with them, and his speed freak friends
> began to hang out there. Alexander Trocchi and his wife,
> Lynn, who had both been shooting speed for years, moved
> in, and the apartment became a shooting gallery. Janine's
> weight dropped to ninety-five pounds. One day she came
> home to find Huncke and Heine gone. They had both
> been arrested. *!!* Elise was carried away to Hillside mental
> hospital, diagnosed as acutely schizophrenic. The terrors
> of the Methedrine plague were beginning to be seen.

So what was this doing in my file? It could have been a joke, of
course. BBC managers have been known to be mischievous. But is your
employment record, even a record that is divided into white/good file
and black/bad file, the proper place for black humour?

Did my bosses think they had discovered a significant
contribution to my CV that I had neglected to mention?
It is just possible, given the date of 23 March, 1961,
that I was a speed freak junkie hanging out with the
likes of Jack Kerouac and Allen Ginsberg. After all I had
just turned sixteen and maybe I was living a double
life – by day a devout Catholic altar boy and cadet at
a Benedictine Military Academy called Marmion, by
night and on holiday, the centre of a drug ring on the
cusp of the Methedrine plague with the Beat Poets in
New York.

'A speed freak junkie?'

Perhaps the BBC really did think somewhere along the line that
they were getting a colourful character who had 'done time' in New
York and done a lot of drugs too. Were my bosses looking for a tame,
reformed addict to give a new perspective to local radio in Oxford?
Well, Auntie Beeb, if that's the case, I'm sorry that I haven't lived up to
your expectations, but you have certainly exceeded mine. Thanks.